From Speculator to Investor

FROM SPECULATOR TO INVESTOR

Dr Qasim Mohammedbhai

First published by Arena Books in 2024
www.arenabooks.co.uk

Qasim Mohammedbhai
From Speculator to Investor

ISBN 978-1-914390-38-8 Paperback
ISBN 978-1-914390-39-5 Ebook

A CIP catalogue record for this book is available from the British Library.

Thema: KFFM; VSB; UDBM; KJ; KFF; KFC; KFCR; KFFS

Cover design by Jelena Mirkovic

For Moiz & Safiyah

CONTENTS

PREFACE

My passion in the stock market began as a teenager. Back then I was naive, I just wanted to drive a Lamborghini and had absolutely no idea what I was doing. I had no basic understanding of the market, I was unable to understand financial news, podcasts, company reports, the list goes on. But as a cocksure teenager I thought I had the 'edge'. When my grandfather gave me money to spend on schoolbooks, I thought I knew better, and after doing a course on day trading, opened an account under my dad's name. I did this without telling him of course, as you weren't legally allowed to open an account until you were eighteen. A few months later, you would never have guessed, I blew it all. Looks like the Lamborghini would have to wait. If only bitcoin and cryptos were out back then…

This was a big hit for me mentally. It definitely set me back and gave me the huge reality check that making money isn't easy. I left my interest in finance behind for a few months, wanting to pretend it didn't happen. However, I was stubborn. I was determined to learn more, so I started reading books from famous investors I had heard of: Warren Buffett, Peter Lynch, Benjamin Graham, Ray Dalio, Howard Marks, Tony Robbins and many more. I read thousands of articles, publications and podcasts to gain a better understanding of investing and its many modalities. I got myself a mentor, and three years later I decided it was time to have another crack. This is where my journey as an INVESTOR truly began.

I am by no means a professional investor and cannot bedazzle you with an extensive list of credentials. I work as a dentist out of London. I look at people's mouths all day, drilling, filling and billing. Despite my sarcasm I love dentistry. That said, I have a greater passion for investing and wealth management, which led me to start my own real estate investment trust. Over the years I have come to appreciate the key differentiator between the wealthy and the poor. Robert Kiyosaki, author of *Rich Dad Poor Dad* puts it excellently: 'Schools teach you how to work for money, but they don't teach you how to make money work for you.' My reason for being an investor is to make my money work hard for me, so I don't have to work hard for it. Less time working is more time living. As one palliative care nurse noted, one of the biggest regrets of the dying was 'I wish I hadn't worked so hard.'

I truly believe that getting your money to work for you should be and can be everyone's goal. The reason for writing this book was to help transform the working class to the investing class; to provide the knowledge to enable people to understand, make decisions, and take control of their own financial future. Even after reading this book you may decide that it's not for you and you wish to give your money to a finance manager. Guess what, that's great! At least now you will be making an informed decision. More than that, you will understand what someone else is doing with your money and your future. The finance industry is notorious for its use of jargon to confuse clients with terms they don't understand. Unfortunately, things that sound elaborate attract people and their money, which is how Wall Street thrives. They are constantly creating and promoting new financial mediums to lure in clients and make sales. Can you name any other profession where you would get away with this? If I tried to confuse my patients with jargon and carried out dental work that they didn't understand, I would get branded a sleazy dentist and get struck off!

A lot of the people handling your money don't care if they win or lose, they still get paid. In fact, the more transactions they carry out, in other words the more stocks they buy and sell, the more they make. In 2020, Fidelity (one of the biggest brokerage firms in America) carried out a survey to find out what type of investors performed the best. They compared sex, age and various other factors. They found that the best characteristic an investor could have was… you'll never guess what, but deceased. Deceased! Why? I hear you asking. Because they were not able to touch their account and use their emotions to make rash decisions and buy and sell. So here we are paying money managers bucket loads in commission to carry out numerous transactions, when the most successful ones are people that can't touch their account.

I'll end with an old adage:

> Once in dear dead days beyond recall, an out-of-town visitor was being shown the wonders of the New York financial district. When the party arrived at the Battery, one of his guides indicated some handsome ships riding at the anchor. He said, "Look, those are the bankers' and the brokers' yachts."
>
> "Where are the customers' yachts?" asked the naïve visitor.
>
> ***Where are the customers' yachts,*** **Fred Schwed Jr**

ACKNOWLEDGEMENTS

With thanks to my loving parents without whose guidance, teachings and inspiration I would not be where I am today. Thanks also to my family for their unconditional love and support. And last but not least, I owe a debt of gratitude to my first mentor, Ali.

Introduction
Be an Emotionless Cyborg

What is an investor? Google came back with this:

> 'An investor is an individual that puts money into an entity such as a business for a financial return. The main goal of any investor is to minimise risk and maximise return. It is in contrast with a speculator who is willing to invest in a risky asset with the hopes of getting a higher profit.'

The key message from this definition is the difference between an investor and a speculator. An investor executes his moves in a calculated manner, whereas a speculator does so with the *hopes of getting a higher profit.* Even if the speculator buys the exact same stock as the investor, without thorough reasoning, exit strategy or risk management it is speculation. Buying Tesla solely because it keeps going up and all your friends are talking about it is speculation. The same goes for AMC and GameStop, despite the well-known Reddit fact that they are 'going to the moon.' My reason for writing this book, if it wasn't evident from the book title, is to turn you from a speculator into an investor. This is not a secret recipe to get rich; it is the start of your journey. It will give you the tools and direction to take you further into whatever style of investing suits your personality and stage in life.

It took me a while to understand what personality had to do with investing. Isn't it just about making sure you make the right calls, buy the right stocks at the right time and sell them when they're up? The reality is that investing is all about decision making and re-evaluating one's decision making. A person's temperament, stress management and emotional state of mind have a huge impact on decision making. An article written in the *Annual Review of Psychology* states that 'Emotions constitute potent, pervasive, predictable, sometimes harmful and sometimes beneficial drivers of decision making.'[1] An example that shocks me still is when judges pass down sentences on days following a loss by the local city's football team, they tend to be tougher than on days following a win. If this topic interests you, an excellent book I recommend you read is *Noise*. It goes into depth about the flaw in human judgement.

Going back to investing, what temperament makes a good investor? Put simply, an emotionless cyborg! Someone who doesn't let their emotions run amok and take the place of sound and logical reasoning. But alas we are human. Will Smith said that "Human beings are not creatures of logic; we are creatures of emotions. And we do not care what's true. We care how it feels." I wonder if he said that before or after he slapped the daylights out of a presenter on live television… Jokes aside, his statement could not be truer. We are not cyborgs, and we have emotions, especially when it comes to money. The conclusion to be drawn is that our emotions need to be managed. If you are someone that is completely risk-averse, then a portfolio of government-backed bonds may be for you. If you are willing to take slightly more risks

---

1 Lerner, J.S. Lerner *et al.* 'Emotion and decision making', *Annual Review of Psychology*, Vol. 66(1), 2015, pp. 799–823. doi:10.1146/annurev-psych-010213-115043.

but still don't want an emotional roller coaster then a defensive portfolio of high-quality stocks and government-backed bonds may be more for you. If you can cope with, and want to take on, more risk, then stocks and options might be better suited. When I was technical trading (a term we will address later), I was checking my charts constantly throughout the day, and the stress would really affect my well-being. Even if I didn't blow all my money, that style of investing was not a good fit for me. Only through practice, experience and mistakes will you find the style that suits your personality.

The second factor that impacts the style of investing you choose is where you are in life. This is more obvious: if you are a ninety-year-old, you are most likely not going to want to have the same portfolio as a twenty-five-year-old. The same goes if you have people that are financially dependent on you, be it your partner, children, or you're managing a pension fund for thousands of employees and their families. Only you can decide how much risk is too much. The quintessential point being that whatever risk you take it is calculated!

> 'Between calculated risk and reckless decision-making lies the dividing line between profit and loss.' Charles Duhigg

Part 1 of this book covers the different financial instruments and explains all the different ways your money can be invested in the market.

Part 2 will go over financial statements, balance sheets and cash flow statements, teaching you how to do a deep dive into the accounts of a company.

Part 3 will cover macroeconomics and economy-wide phenomena, things you will hear about in the news, namely inflation, interest rates and market cycles.

Part 4 ties the previous chapters together. Part 4, where we will address investing stratagem, recaps the concepts discussed in the aforementioned chapters, while helping you find your investing niche.

The book is densely packed with financial terms, all of which are explained in great detail. As a dentist, I am constantly having to explain technical terms to patients, so it's something that I am good at. I've found that analogies are very helpful, and I have used a lot in Part 1 and Part 2 to help you get a grip of the fundamentals. I have also included lots of real examples and charts, so you can visualise and apply these teachings to real-life scenarios. The reason I use so much technical lingo is that I want you to be able to engage with the financial world. To do so you have to understand the language they use. When I started, I could never understand financial news programmes, not because it was particularly complex, but because there was so much jargon! If at any time you forget what any of these terms mean, don't worry, I have included a glossary at the back to help. I have also included task sections at various intervals throughout the book. Please try your best to do these. Not only by learning but by doing an action will it be fully cemented in the brain and then be able to be implemented. I know it is very easy to skip over these, but if you put in the time to complete these you will get much more out of the book.

Every chapter has been read by non-finance people, to make sure the topics are well explained and make sense. The one thing some readers struggled to grasp was the mathematics within some of the chapters. I've tried to explain the mathematics as simply as I could, but despite that, some of the readers struggled to understand it all. If you do struggle with mathematics, then please don't worry about not fully getting some of those sections. There are plenty of websites that can do the maths for you. For those of you that do struggle a bit with maths, by understanding the significance of the number, you can get away with not understanding how to calculate it.

As you progress through the book, you will develop a profound understanding of what it means to be an investor, and what investing can offer you. I am confident that you will see its potential, as well as its versatility, enabling you to create a bespoke platform to achieve your financial goals.

PART 1

INVESTMENT SECURITIES

A security is defined as 'a thing deposited or pledged as a guarantee of the fulfilment of an undertaking or the repayment of a loan, to be forfeited in case of default.' As explained here, it would be something that functions as a guarantee in case a person isn't able to pay back a loan. It was seen as a safety net of sorts for institutions that lend money. An example is Vijay Mallya, a billionaire who planned to go on holiday for two weeks. He borrowed $5,000 from a bank. In return, he handed over the keys to his Rolls-Royce as security. If he defaulted on the repayment, the bank would keep the Rolls-Royce. As it happens, he came back two weeks later, paid back the $5,000 plus the $15 of interest generated. I'm sure the two questions going through your mind are: why did he give his Rolls-Royce, worth sixty times more, as collateral? And why does a billionaire need to borrow $5,000? When the bank manager asked him this, he said: "Where else in New York City can I park my car for two weeks for $15!"

As you can see, securities are treated as an asset. An asset being an object which is a store of value. So what is an investment security? Investment securities are any tradable financial assets that are purchased with the intention of holding them for an investment. The reason I use the word securities is that firstly, you will come across the term being used in the investing world, and more importantly, I want us to start looking at buying stocks and bonds as investment assets, not just items of speculation! We are buying assets and thus securities. Real estate and property are seen as more robust securities, hence why it is much easier to borrow money by taking out a mortgage. Investment securities, however, can also be used as collateral. Look at Elon Musk, he has recently bought X, formerly Twitter, in his crusade against censorship and promoting freedom of speech. He used his $62.5 billion worth of Tesla stock as security, for a $12.5 billion loan to help him purchase the company. Of course, only the ultra-wealthy get to do this, but the point I'm trying to get across is that when we buy a stock, we OWN an ASSET. In Part 1 of this book, we are going to go over the two main categories of securities: equities and bonds.

Chapter 1
Equities & Dividends

Equities

Equities and stocks are practically synonymous terms. They both represent ownership of a company. The difference being that a stock is equity that is tradable (equities may or may not be tradable), meaning we can buy and sell stocks through public stock exchanges. When we buy a stock, we own an equity interest in that company. The company's assets, goodwill and products belong to us. If you buy a share of Amazon, you are an owner of Amazon. It doesn't qualify you to start calling yourself Jeff, but legally, if the company makes a profit, you are entitled to that profit as a shareholder (you may not get to decide what to do with it, but the profits belong to the share that you own). If that company goes bankrupt, once it's paid its debts the remainder of its assets belong to you.

If you are an investor and you buy a stock, you should be thinking to yourself, is this a business I want to own? If so, the next question is, at what price do I want to own this business? As Warren Buffett said: "Buy into a company because you want to own it, not because you want the stock to go up."

Let's go back a bit and find out why a company releases its

shares to the public in the first place. When a company wants to raise money, it can do so in two ways. Debt or equity. By taking on debt, the company has to pay it back, with interest, exactly like when we take out a loan. It can raise debt by borrowing from a bank, or by selling bonds (see Chapter 2).

With equity, the company doesn't have to pay it back, but it gives up ownership of the company. You can sell equity on the private or public market. Selling equity privately can be to private investors, financial institutions or venture capital firms (VC firms). Most VC firms invest in up-and-coming businesses, which they believe have significant growth potential. These are often companies early in their journey who don't have the track record to secure funding from banks, and have to sell part of their company (sell equity). A good example of this are the TV shows *Dragons' Den* for the UK or *Shark Tank* for the US. An entrepreneur comes to the "Dragons" or "Sharks," who represent the private investors. The entrepreneur then offers a 'stake' (equity) in their company for a sum of money (capital).

To raise money publicly, a company would sell their equity through a stock exchange. This can be the New York Stock Exchange (NYSE) or the London Stock Exchange (LSE), and the list goes on. To be listed on an exchange, they have to be properly audited, their accounts have to be in order and they have to comply with the SEC's rules (Securities and Exchange Commission – the police of the stock market). Once approved, the company becomes available to the public as an IPO. This stands for an initial public offering, where the shares are first listed on the market and are available to be bought. The company gives up ownership, in return for shareholders' equity (money which comes from shareholders' purchases of its shares). This money can then be used by the company for whatever it wishes.

When buying a share of the exchange, you wouldn't buy it directly. It would be through a broker. The days of phoning your broker to buy a stock is very old school. Now it's all automated and can be done through your phone in a few taps. You are still going through a broker, but it is an online one. Normally the broker charges you a commission to place the order, and sometimes a small fee to hold the share in your account. There are many new brokers out there that don't charge any commission! One of them is Robin Hood, aptly named unless you know about the GameStop scandal. Many of these commission-free companies are only available to US citizens, but there are some out there for UK investors too. For those of you that are technophobic, you can call your broker in person and they can process the investment transaction for you. However, they may charge a slightly higher fee for this.

A stock on the market has two prices. A bid price and an ask price. The bid price is the highest price a buyer will pay for a security, whereas the ask price is the lowest price a seller will accept for a security. If you were to buy a security, you would pay the ask price, which is the lowest price a seller will sell it to you. If you are selling your security, you would sell at the bid price, which is the highest a buyer will pay you. The ask price is always higher than the bid price, and the difference between the two is called the Bid-Ask spread. It is like supply and demand, the bid being the demand, and the ask being the supply. Let's use an example to clarify things. Apple's ask price is $148.00. If you were to buy the stock, this is the lowest someone will sell it to you. Apple's bid price is $147.85. This is the highest you can get if you sell your holding. The Bid-Ask spread being 15p, or in percentage terms = 0.1%. This means that if you buy and sell your Apple shares instantaneously (assuming no commission fees), you will lose 0.1% on the spread between the ask and bid price. This is Apple, a security which has lots of supply and lots of demand. With lots of both, you will get a narrow Bid-Ask spread. This is good for us investors, as we essentially pay less transaction-associated fees.

A stock with a narrow bid and ask price has good liquidity. Liquidity can be defined as the ease with which an asset can be converted into cash. Take the Forex market as an example. This is where currencies are exchanged for other currencies. It's cash for cash, they are the most liquid of assets by definition. The percentage spread between bid and ask for GPB/USD (the pound to the dollar) is 0.008%.

On the other side of the scale is a stock like Base Resources. It is a company which owns a well-run mine in Kenya, and pays out huge amounts to its shareholders in profits. Its percentage spread is 3%. It comes as no surprise that the demand for a mine in Kenya is far inferior than Apple Inc. We the investors pay the price for this, a steep price, no doubt.

In the midst of a sudden market crash, for example the Great Crash of 1929, the two big down days, Black Monday and Black Tuesday, saw huge dips in the market over two consecutive days. On these days there was a rush of sellers, but no one willing to buy the stock. So, the bid price (price someone is willing to pay to buy a stock) plummets and so does the ask price (price someone is willing to sell the stock). In this way the price of the stock crashes, leaving investors selling their shares at a much lower valuation. On Black Monday alone, the Dow Jones Index lost nearly 22% in a single day. This would be considered a huge move for a major index, even if it happened over a year. This took place in just one day!

Dividends

You've just bought your first equity and now you are an owner of that company. If the company makes a profit, that profit belongs to your share. Even though it belongs to your share, you most likely won't get much say in what to do with the profits, as this is down to the company's management. There are two thing a company can do with the money. They can either keep it, or distribute it to shareholders. If they choose to distribute a portion of the profits to the shareholders, then it is called a dividend payment. It is important to note that the company has no obligation to pay out a dividend.

We as shareholders have a right to expect that if the company chooses not to pay out a dividend and to keep the money it is spent in a productive way which will increase shareholder equity. This means that whatever they do, they do something that will ultimately lead to growth in the company, resulting in an increase in share price, thus an increase in asset value. As the asset or equity (the share) we hold becomes more valuable, it can be sold for a higher price. This is why when buying into a company it's important that there is a good management team, one that spends our cash wisely, leading to an increase in profits and hence an increase in share price. We will talk more about this in Chapter 4.

If a company does decide to share the profits with the shareholders, and pay a dividend, then it tends to spread them out at certain points during the year. Look at Figure 1:1, which is the dividend history of Royal Dutch Shell in 2020. It spread out its dividends over four different dates during the year, Q1–Q4. 'Q' refers to the quarters of the year, so every quarter represents three months. Most companies also release financial statements every quarter to keep their shareholders informed about the company's progress. The date that the money is paid out for these four quarters is listed in the payment date column. However, to be eligible for a dividend payment on those dates, you must own the stock before the specified 'Ex-dividend date.' This date works as a deadline of sorts, and as you can see from Figure 1:1, it is around a month before the dividend gets paid out. All companies' dividend dates can be easily found by typing them into Google. Give it a go now…

TASK – Find the next dividend date and amount for the oil company BP.

2020	Ex-Dividend Date	Payment Date	GB Pence
Q4	18/02/2021	29/03/2021	11.96
Q3	12/11/2020	16/12/2020	12.48
Q2	13/08/2020	21/09/2020	12.09
Q1	14/05/2020	22/06/2020	12.68

Figure 1:1: Royal Dutch Shell dividend history

Dividend payments are expressed as an amount per share. The most important thing isn't the amount, but the comparison of the amount to the share price. We call this the dividend yield, and it is expressed as a percentage. The dividend yield gives you your return on investment. Look at it like buying a flat to rent. In the analogy, the rent is the dividend, and the flat is the share you bought. So, if you have a flat rental that pays you a yield of 5%, then the rental amount is 5% of what you bought the house for. So it will take you twenty years to pay off the house with rent alone (5% x 20 = 100%). Let's get back to equities and use National Grid as our example. They come under the utilities sector, as they are the world's largest provider of electricity and gas, operating in the UK and US. They are a very safe company, which generates a consistent profit, and decide to distribute this to their shareholders. They are scheduled to pay two dividends this year, one being their mid-year dividend of 17.21p a share, and the other their end-of-year dividend of 33.76p a share. This adds up to a yearly payment of 50.97p. The price of the National Grid share is around 1032p.

To calculate the annual dividend yield:

$$Dividend\ Yield = \frac{Total\ yearly\ dividend}{Share\ price} \times 100\%$$

To plug in the numbers from National Grid:

$$National\ Grid\ Dividend\ Yield = \frac{17.21 + 33.76}{1032} \times 100\% = 4.9\%$$

So, the annual dividend yield is calculated by dividing the dividend over the share price, and multiplying it by 100 to arrive at a percentage. This gives us a dividend yield of 4.9%. If the maths is confusing or it's too much effort, then you can find dividend yield very easily by googling it or by using financial sites like Yahoo Finance or even the stocks app on your iPhone.

TASK – Calculate or search using Yahoo Finance the dividend yield for Leggett & Platt.

Buying a stock for its dividend payment is a very legitimate strategy, and one that can provide a dependable form of income, as it constitutes a regular payment year on year. There are three things we want to see from a good dividend payer:

1. **Good dividend history**
   By this, we want to see many years of dividends being paid without fail. The longer the history the better.
2. **Good dividend cover**
   Dividend cover relates to how easily a company can pay a dividend. A company that only makes just enough money a year to cover the dividend might not be able to make future payments if they hit hard times. This may lead them to cut the dividend, reducing the amount paid, or just not paying out a dividend at all. If a company is paying too high a dividend,

be wary, and make sure they can afford to do so.

3.   **Increasing dividend**
This last one isn't necessarily a must, though a good company ideally should have a steady growth. More growth of profits means more to hand out to shareholders, hence the higher dividend payments.

In Chapter 12 we look in more depth at how to analyse a stock for dividend investment, and we will go through an example from my own portfolio.

For now, let's look at an oil company: Royal Dutch Shell. Below is a graph of eighteen years showing the stock price and the dividend price. One of the things that attracted me was the dividend payouts. When I bought the company in 2019, they had not cut the dividend since World War II, which is an amazing dividend history! Furthermore, if you look at the second graph, the dividend payout has undergone a steady increase for sixteen of the eighteen years. This is despite the fluctuations in the stock price that you can see above. The management are clearly hell-bent on paying dividends and increasing dividend. You can't blame me for thinking that the only thing on the horizon that would stop these guys paying a dividend was World War III. Unlucky for me, COVID hit, and the demand for oil dropped massively as people weren't driving. This led to the management deciding to heavily reduce the dividends and keep more money in the company's coffers. Not to spend, mind you, but to store as a rainy-day fund. The dividend has steadily been on the rise again from the bottom during COVID. While COVID threw a spanner in the works, Royal Dutch Shell is an example of a dividend-paying company with a good dividend history, dividend cover and increasing dividend payments.

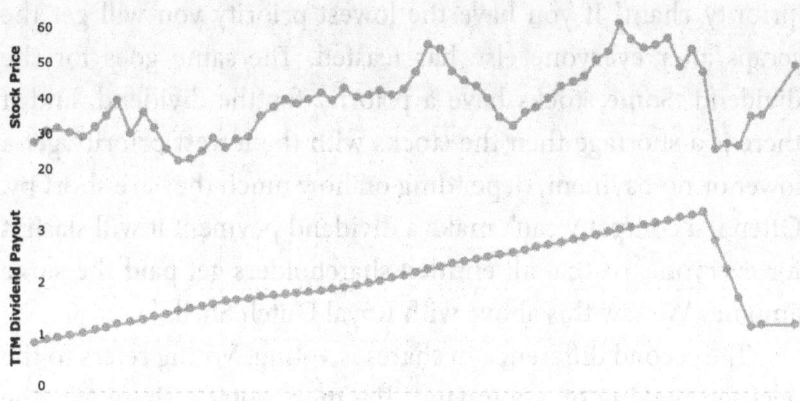

Figure 1:2: Royal Dutch Shell – Stocks and Dividends over the last 18 years.

Some companies really spoil their shareholders and pay out a special dividend. This is a dividend paid out in addition to the other dividends given. Companies may choose to do so when they have had an excellent financial year and choose to reward their shareholders. Let's go back to National Grid, who pay a dividend yield of around 5%. In 2017 they announced that they would pay a special dividend of around 7.5%. This is 7.5% on top of the 5% they normally pay.

Equity Classes

We've talked a lot about buying a share in a company as being synonymous with ownership of a company. This is still true, but there is a hierarchy of ownership that needs to be understood. When a company goes public, it may create different types or classes of shares. The most notable differences are priority and voting rights.

The first difference in share classes, priority, refers to who get 'dibs' on the company's assets. This comes about when the company goes bankrupt and the assets get allocated along the

19

'priority chain.' If you have the lowest priority you will get the scraps after everyone else has feasted. The same goes for the dividend. Some stocks have a priority for the dividend, and if there is a shortage then the stocks with the lowest priority get a lower or no payment, depending on how much they are short by. Often if a company can't make a dividend payment it will slash it for everyone, so that all entitled shareholders get paid the same amount. We saw this above with Royal Dutch Shell.

The second difference in shares is voting. Voting refers to the decision making of a company. The more votes a share has, the more control you as a shareholder have over what the company does. This is useful for owners of a privately owned company that take their company public but still want to call the shots. They can ensure that they own the shares that have more voting rights. Let's go over some examples of share classes and it will make more sense. There are two main categories of shares: common shares and preferred shares.

COMMON SHARES

Common shares can take the form of Class A, B or C shares. Now, a company will state which shares take precedence, and what entitlements they have. This can be priority for dividends, assets (in case of bankruptcy) or for voting rights. Normally, Class A shares are ranked higher than Class B and so on with Class C. This is not always the case as we will see below.

Take the company Berkshire Hathaway. They have Class A and Class B shares. The difference between these classes is in the voting rights, referring to an investor's say in the affairs of the company. One Class A share has 10,000 votes, whereas one Class B share has one vote, a significant difference. Bear in mind, one Class A share costs $440,000, whereas a Class B share costs $300. This is the price you pay if you want to have a say in what a company that holds $39 billion in cash does. It is worth mentioning that one share of Class A can be converted into 1,500 Class B shares. It's not like you paying hundreds of thousands just for voting rights. The reason they keep the price so high is because it acts as a minimum that one must invest, as a show of commitment to the company. Many Class A shares aren't sold publicly anyway even if you wanted to buy them. For Berkshire Hathaway the conversion only goes one way; you can't convert 1,500 B shares into A shares.

Another company with a different make-up is Alphabet, otherwise known as Google. They have a multi-class structure made up of three shares, A, B and C. Class A shares are given to regular investors and have one vote per share. Class B shares are held only by the two owners of Google and have ten votes per share. Class C shares on the other hand have no votes per share and are held by the employees of the company. This example shows that it is not always the case that Class A shares have more voting rights. It may be worth checking the equity structure of a company before investing.

Just because a company's shares are more expensive doesn't mean the company is more valuable. It all depends on how many times the company has chosen to split itself up. As an example, Microsoft shares are priced at $300, but they have 7 billion shares. We can create a company now with a share price of $500 dollars with only one share. If we split it up into 7 billion shares like Microsoft, then the new share price would be but a fraction of a penny.

If the share price increases significantly, it can get so expensive per share that people can't afford to buy a share. The company may choose to perform a stock split (Microsoft have undergone nine stock splits since conception). So, if Company A have a stock worth £1,000, they may split every share into ten parts (called ten 10-for-1 split) – this means all shares are now £100. This makes them more affordable for investors that want to spend less than £1,000 on Company A. Technically, one share is less valuable now. However, if you had £1,000 invested in Company A, before the stock split you would own one share worth £1,000, and after it, you would have ten shares worth £100 each (ten shares totalling £1,000). There's no difference in your actual value, it just means you have more flexibility. Let's say the stock went up by 40%, and you wanted to bank some profits and sell half of the shares. Now that you have ten shares, you can sell five. Before the stock split you only had one, so you couldn't do your own private stock split and sell half a share. As we discussed above, Warren Buffett's company, Berkshire Hathaway, have not split their Class A shares, which have a worth of $440,000 per share! Buffett has intentionally kept this in order to attract investors who stay with the company for the long term, not short-term traders.

NB – The next section on preferred shares may get a little confusing. The best way to describe them is the halfway house between common shares and bonds. We haven't gone over bonds yet as that is coming soon in Chapter 2. If you are struggling to understand it, it will make more sense once you read Chapter 2.

PREFERRED SHARES

Preferred shares are an equity class which, as the name 'preferred' suggests, gets precedence over the common shares for dividend payments. Dividend payments would go to the preferred shares first, before going to the common shares. In the event of a bankruptcy, preferred shareholders' claim to assets is above that of the common shareholders. Normally, preferred shares receive a fixed dividend. By this I mean a fixed amount per share, whereas dividends for the common share can vary, as we saw in the example above. Some preferred shares are known as participating shares. This entitles the holder to be paid above the fixed rate, should the common shareholders receive a dividend above the one paid to the preferred shareholders.

Preferred shares are not valued in the same way as common shares. They have what is called a par value, which we will examine in Chapter 2 when we discuss bonds. For now, understand that they do not move with the common stock, and do not provide the same opportunities for growth as normal shares do. If a common stock increases by 50% you will most certainly not see this for preferred stock. If you are investing in a company for its growth, then you should buy common shares. If you are investing for dividend, then preferred shares might be a good option.

Cumulative vs non-cumulative

A cumulative preferred share entitles the holder to be paid dividends, including payments that are missed. These would build up, like a tab of sorts, and must be paid before the common share receives any dividend. Non-cumulative shares do not have the ability to 'claim' missed dividend payments.

Convertible

Convertible shares allow the holder to convert their preferred shares into common stock should they wish. Some convertibles have provisions which allow the company to force conversion of preferred to common stock. With convertible stock, its price often follows the price of the common share, as its convertibility creates a link between the two classes. The benefit of a convertible preferred share is that one is able to get a fixed dividend, and benefit from any increase in common stock share price, as it can convert to common stock and then sell the shares.

For example, Company Y sells its preferred convertible share at £100. It is convertible into five shares of common Class A stock. Meaning that it costs us £20 per share (£100 divided by the number of shares we receive if we convert $= \frac{100}{5} = £20$). If the price of the common share were to increase to £30 a share, we could convert our preferred share to five common shares, then profit from the increase in share price. If we converted, we would get five shares worth £150. On our initial investment of £100, our profit would equal £50, meaning we made a 50% gain on our initial £100 investment.

Bear in mind that the convertible share prices are linked to common share price, so when the common share increases, so does the convertible share price. It may not be necessary to actively convert to common shares to make a profit, as the price of the convertible share may increase to £150 following the increase in the common share.

Chapter 2
Investment Securities – Bonds

The first way to raise money is by selling equity, which we covered in the previous chapter. A company would give up equity, that is, ownership of the company, in return for capital (money). This is money that DOESN'T have to be paid back. The other way a company can raise capital is by taking on debt. We take on debt through mortgages, bank loans etc. Companies have an additional vehicle called bonds. Companies can sell bonds, promising the buyer of the bond a fixed return (a percentage yield, like we discussed in our preferred stock), and a maturity date (an expiry date), whereby the company must pay the bond holder the full value of the bond.

In simple terms, we are lending the company money (by buying the bond). The company pays us interest on this borrowed money (the fixed return or yield) and pays us back the money we lent on a predetermined date (maturity date). The fixed yield is given as a percentage in the same way dividends are. They are known as coupons. For example, Microsoft issues bonds with a

3.3% coupon, maturing in 2027. This means Microsoft will pay 3.3% on your investment every year, and pay you back the full price of investment in 2027.

The fundamental difference between a dividend and a bond is that the latter represents a legally binding commitment from the company to pay its bondholder the specified yield. It cannot decide not to pay out, like a company can when it pays dividends. If a company cannot pay its debts, it goes into bankruptcy. In the event of bankruptcy, the bondholder has a claim to that company's assets. They have a HIGHER priority than the shareholders. This means that when the company is liquidated (its assets turned to cash to pay its debtors and shareholders in bankruptcy), the bondholders get paid first. If there is anything left then this is distributed to the shareholders. Look it at this way, when we purchase an equity, we agree to take on the company's responsibilities. If the company has taken on debt, that debt belongs to all the owners. Hence, it's the owners (or in this case the shareholders) that have to pay off the debts before taking anything for themselves. The same applies for dividend payments. A company will only pay out a dividend if it can cover its interest payments on its debt. This brings us back to the second point for picking a dividend-paying stock outlined in Chapter 1: its dividend cover. When calculating dividend cover, we have to factor in how much debt the company has taken on, as these debt repayments will be paid first. As mentioned earlier, we will cover this in more detail in Chapter 12.

Bonds are priced differently to stocks, they do not have wildly different prices and have much less fluctuation. This is because a bond simply represents a nominal figure, which we call the 'par value.' This figure represents the borrowed amount. The price of a bond fluctuates depending on a company's ability to pay its debt, not necessarily on its performance or growth like a stock does. The price of bonds revolves around this par value.

This is the nominal amount that the company will pay back to you on maturation of the bond. Bonds can trade below or above the par value, depending on a company's credit rating. The credit rating, which we will discuss below, will indicate how likely the company is to sustain its debt payments. If a company it at a risk of defaulting on its debts, it will likely trade sub-par, at a value below its par value. Even if it trades at below par, upon maturity (the expiry date of the bonds), the company is legally obliged to pay you par value. Par value is normally set at $1,000; however, the UK government sells its bonds at a par value of £100. The reason being, to make it more affordable for the average household.

Let's use a hypothetical scenario to explain the difference between stocks and bonds. For example, Company A has earnings of x, and its income is twenty times the amount of its debt repayments. This is a company that's very unlikely to default on payments, so its bond price will be around par. Let's say the next year, the company doubles its earnings. The stock would rocket, as this company is a very fast-growing company, with good future prospects, so the company becomes more valuable. This is because value is derived from a company's earnings and potential future earnings. As the earnings of a company increase, especially at such an aggressive rate, it suggests more growth is on the horizon, so your stock becomes worth more. Its bond, on the other hand, would not change much. This is because as a bondholder you don't own the company. At twenty times the income, no one's worried that the bond payments won't be fulfilled, so the bond will be around par value. If the earnings double, and the bond payments equal forty times the income, then of course we are less worried about default, though we weren't worried in the first place. The bond will still stay at par, as there is not much reason for it to go above par. If the company pays a dividend, it may choose to increase the dividend as a reward to the owners as the earnings have doubled. But bondholder aren't owners, they are lenders, so no company is going to give more than the fixed yield to their bondholders. In the same way we don't give extra as a tip to the bank when paying back our mortgage! In this scenario, there won't be much change in the bond value, although there will be a significant change in the share value. Now let's say the earnings the following year drop by 25%. This will take the earnings to thirty times the bond payments. Guess what, we still aren't worried about the company making the bond repayments so the bond price will still be at par. The stock price, however, will drop, as they were expecting the astronomical growth from the previous year to continue. This is a hypothetical scenario, but it demonstrates that even though stock prices may vary, bond prices may remain stable. What also stabilises bonds is their maturation date, by which time a set par value will be paid to the bondholder.

Bonds are undoubtedly a safer and less volatile security than stocks. They have the added benefit of stable and consistent returns. Going back to our ninety-year-old man, you can see how bonds might be an attractive investment vehicle for him to continue his retirement.

In general, the safest bonds are government bonds, also known as municipal bonds. As the name suggests, these are bonds you buy from the government. When the person that owes you is the government, it's going to take a lot for them not to pay out. Even more than COVID... Now, obviously it depends on the government, as some countries do default on their bonds. Spain defaulted fifteen times between the eighteenth and nineteenth centuries, Ukraine defaulted on $117 billion in 2020 and Sri Lanka defaulted on $51 billion this year. So not all countries are safe, but for ones like the US or UK, the country has to collapse before they default on your bond payments. And if they do collapse, your investment portfolio will be the least of your worries.

Ratings

We have spoken about the safety and security of bonds; however, this is not the full story. Bonds have ratings, and these ratings are based on the ability of a company to honour their debt obligations. It's essentially a credit rating. A few companies do it, one of them being Standard & Poor's, the same people that make the S&P 500 Index. Another popular one is Moody's Investors Service. For S&P's ratings, they range from AAA to D, AAA being the best credit rating and D being the worst. Anything from AAA to BBB- is considered 'investment grade.' From BB+ to D, it is considered 'speculative.' Speculative bonds are also known as 'junk bonds.' Take a look at the table below which will explain the ratings. The lower the ratings, the lower the ability to pay debtors, and the higher the chance of default. However, with more risk comes more reward. For companies that receive lower ratings, they have to make themselves more attractive to investors, so they offer higher yields on their bonds. Believe it or not, the renowned car company Ford is rated BB+, which is classed as a speculative or junk bond. This low rating means they pay a high yield of 8.875%. Compare this to Apple Inc., rated AAA, an extremely strong investment grade. This bond has a coupon of 3%. Compare this to the UK municipal bonds, which pay a yield of 2.19%. You can see that as the credit quality of a bond increases, the yield decreases. Like I said before, the greater the risk, the greater the reward. Investing in junk bonds is hard, and not only requires a deep understanding of businesses, but excellent judgement. The safest way to invest in junk bonds is through a junk bond Exchange-Traded Fund (ETF), which is something you can buy that contains hundreds of junk bonds. This way you can diversify, so if one company goes into liquidation, you have plenty of others to pick up the slack. We will cover ETFs in more detail in Chapter 3.

Letter Grade	Grade	Capacity to Repay
AAA	Investment	Extremely strong
AA+, AA, AA-	Investment	Very strong
A+, A, A-	Investment	Strong
BBB+, BBB, BBB-	Investment	Adequate
BB+, BB	Speculative	Faces major future uncertainties
B	Speculative	Faces major uncertainties
CCC	Speculative	Currently vulnerable
CC	Speculative	Currently highly vulnerable
C	Speculative	Has filed bankruptcy petition
D	Speculative	In default

Figure 2:1: Sample ratings table.

Distressed Debt Investing

Investing in distressed debt is buying the bonds of companies that are in financial difficulty. These bonds are trading at a significant discount from par. You can make money if the companies make a turnaround, honouring the bond repayments and payback on maturity. In this way you earn yield from a higher coupon rate (with it being a junk bond and paying higher yields), and also make the difference from what you bought the bond for and par value. Let's say you buy a distressed bond of a company rate CC, with a par value of £1,000. It is selling for a 50% discount from its par value (£500 per bond) and has a 10% coupon (which is high as the company has a low bond rating). If you invest £1,000, with a year until maturity, you will receive £100 from the coupon repayment (10% of £1,000), and you will receive another £1,000 when the bond matures at par value. Note that the coupon is a percentage of the par value, not the current bond price. To summarise, from a £500 investment, you have made £600 in profit (the £100 from the 10% bond yield and the £500 on maturity of bond). This comes to a 120% return. If you compare this to our measly 2.19% government return, I'm sure your eyes are flashing green at the thought of distressed debt.

If this was so easy, everyone would do it. What is more likely in this scenario is that the company goes into bankruptcy, you don't get your interest payments or your payment of the bond at maturity. Instead, you get whatever the company can salvage from liquidating their assets when they declare bankruptcy. This is the second way to make money. If the company have assets they can liquidate (turn to cash) that are worth more than the value of the bond you buy, you can make money from the difference. This requires a deep understanding of balance sheets, which we will cover in Chapter 5. You will need to do more research, however, to be successful in distressed investing. Distressed bond investing is not something I would recommend. If you are just embarking on your investment journey, you should avoid it like the plague.

Chapter 3
Indices and ETFs

An index is a tool used to monitor the performance of a group of assets. They can track the economic market as a whole or a more niche sector of the market. The most famous example is the S&P 500 Index, which tracks the biggest 500 US companies. In the UK we have the FTSE 100, which tracks the UK's 100 biggest companies. They are both examples of more general indices. A more niche index is the NASDAQ, which contains technology stocks only. An index can be used as a benchmark for the economy, for the general performance of the stock market or bond market and for passive investing, which we cover in Chapter 12. Note that indices cannot be invested in directly, but can be bought indirectly through ETFs.

ETFs stand for Exchange-Traded Funds. They are an easy and affordable way for an investor to diversify their investments. An ETF can contain many types of investments, be it stocks, bonds etc. It can own hundreds of stocks or bonds spanning a number of industries. The first-ever ETF created was the SPDR S&P 500 ETF. This ETF contains all the stocks within the S&P 500 Index, allowing an individual to invest in this index. As an investor let's say you want to invest in corporate US, wanting to have a stake in all 500 companies in the S&P 500. This would cost you a lot, having to buy at least one stock of every company, let alone the time it would take to go through and buy all 500 companies. The easier and more affordable thing to do would be to buy the SPDR S&P 500 ETF. One would buy this in the same way they buy a stock, through their online broker. By doing so, you get to participate in all 500 stocks, when the S&P 500 goes up, so does your ETF, and when it goes down, the same applies to your ETF. ETFs can also represent baskets of stocks concentrated in a particular sector or industry. If you wanted to invest in the technology sector, then there is an ETF which replicates the NASDAQ index. ETFs like the ones mentioned above are known as passive ETFs. In other words, they simply track the index they are pegged to and have no individual or financial institution making decisions on the contents of the ETF.

Not all ETFs are pegged to indices, and some can represent a group of stocks picked by an individual or financial institution. These are actively managed ETFs, and represent more of the trying to 'pick the best stocks' mentality. For example, in the technology sector, instead of picking the NASDAQ Index you could invest in the ARK Innovation ETF, which is mentioned below. This is a group of tech stocks picked by Cathie Wood and her team of researchers at ARK. This does not contain nearly as many stocks as the NASDAQ, nor are the companies as established as the ones contained in the NASDAQ. Hence this ETF carries more risk, but there is more chance of reward. The theory is that a 'good stock picker' should ideally generate a higher return than the indices. If they don't then what is the point of investing in them when your money is much safer in ETFs that track indices? Some argue that investing in indices is the best way to invest. We will talk about a strategy called 'dollar cost averaging' in Chapter 12.

ETFs can be used to follow certain strategies or ideas. If you are an investor who wants to generate returns through bonds or dividends, then there are ETFs for these. If you want to invest in a new innovation then are ETFs for this too. If you wanted to bet on the price of gold going up, but wanted to do more than just buy physical gold, you could buy a gold ETF, which provides you with exposure to a range of companies who are beneficiaries of increasing gold prices. Currently I am looking at the potential of 3D printing, which is growing by leaps and bounds especially in dentistry. I see a big future in this for other industries. However, I wasn't sure where to start, as I don't know enough about the 3D printing space. To get around this, I am researching 3D printing ETFs, which will diversify my holdings by owning a basket of stock within the 3D printing space. This allows me to profit from this technology without having to commit lots of capital and buy lots of stocks individually, or having to try and pick the best couple of stocks. Currently there are more than 8,000 ETFs. All one has to do is put some securities together and sell the ETF to investors. For this reason, some due diligence is still required when choosing an actively managed ETF. There are plenty of reputable firms who offer high-quality products; iShares ETFs are ones I have used multiple times.

TASK – Go onto the iShares website and browse the different ETFs available

As you can see, the applications of ETFs are innumerable, and can be used for every conceivable strategy. The downside to ETFs is that there is an additional management fee to hold an ETF. Actively managed ETFs usually charge more than passive tracking ETFs, which makes sense as you're paying a premium for their research and decision making in picking the investments within their ETF. To give you an example, the Vanguard S&P 500 ETF charges an annual fee of 0.03%. So for every £1,000, you pay

30p. A very small price to pay for access to the top 500 stocks in the United States. The actively managed ARK innovation ETF on the other hand charges 0.75%, a big difference. I don't want you to focus too much on strategies yet, however, as this will become clearer in Part 4 of the book. The take-home message is that ETFs are a cheap and effective way to capture the returns on broad sectors of the market, reduce your risk and diversify your portfolio.

FROM SPECULATOR TO INVESTOR

Chapter 4
Leveraging Instruments – ETFs, Warrants and Options

There are plenty of financial instruments out there for investors. Why wouldn't there be! It is in the best interest of the people selling these to do so. The more investors buy them, the more commission they get. For this reason, the complexity of financial tools has only increased, giving us investors more choice. In this chapter we will go over higher-risk strategies. As ever, with higher risk comes the sweet promise of a higher reward. To understand these risks, we have to first understand leverage. Personally, when it comes to investing, I do not use leverage. It's a higher-risk strategy which is not for me. I recommend that if you do engage in leverage, you do so judiciously.

Leveraging is the use of debt to amplify investment returns. By using debt and borrowing money, we are able to invest more, and amplify our return on investments. This is all hunky-dory when it goes in our favour, though when it goes against you, your losses are amplified. For example, let's say you own $20k and decide to buy a bitcoin. Bitcoin doubles to $40k and you make

$20k – a 100% gain, that's not bad! At this point we are wishing that we'd put more money in. If we went back in time, we could remortgage our house, giving us $200k, and buy ten bitcoins (at $20k a piece), then if it doubled, we would still make the same gain of 100%, but we would make $200k instead! The opposite is also true, with a slight kicker. If bitcoin halved from $20k to $10k, a 50% loss, without leverage we would lose $10k, and with leverage we would lose $100k. The kicker being that even after the $100k loss, we now have to think about the interest payments generated on the borrowed $200k that has just halved. Conversely, without leverage, although bitcoin halving is a gut punch, at least the $10k loss is finite. If you're thinking no one is stupid enough to use leverage to invest in bitcoin, a very volatile asset, then think again.

The estimated leverage ratio for bitcoin is at 0.22. This means that for every £1 invested in bitcoin, 22p is leveraged. If that isn't crazy enough, the CEO of FTX Exchange has listed a 20x leveraged bitcoin ETF on the Vienna Stock Exchange. That means that whatever gain or loss bitcoin has is multiplied twenty times! When a company has taken on too much debt, we worry about it declaring bankruptcy. The same goes for cryptocurrency, but replace the word bankruptcy with collapse. If the bitcoin price falls, these investors levered up to their eyeballs will at some point have to sell, as they can't afford to lose more. They have to sell their positions and cut their losses, as they physically can't afford for bitcoin to fall more. Often, they don't have a choice, as the financial institution will force sell it for them. This is called being 'margin called.' To explain this, we will use one of the biggest advocates of bitcoin, Michael Saylor, owner of MicroStrategy. His firm has spent $4 billion on bitcoin. He has borrowed money from the banks to do so. When borrowing, the bank requests a security for collateral in the event of default on payment. The collateral that MicroStrategy has put down will take them until bitcoin hits a price of $21k, at which price Saylor will be margin called, thus forced to sell, or put down more collateral. What happens if Michael Saylor doesn't want to put down more collateral, or if MicroStrategy don't have more collateral to put down? Then he will be margin called, and forced to sell the 129,218 coins that they own. This will cause a drop in the price of bitcoin. What happens when this drop triggers more margin calls belonging to other leveraged positions? The answer is that we get a mass market sell-off, as we trigger more margin calls until we hit rock bottom. The ironic thing with this case is that the collateral that MicroStrategy used was bitcoin. So the bank accepted bitcoin as collateral to allow them to buy more bitcoin! This is exactly how the bank and housing market crash of 2008 happened. The banks gave out loans on collateral which wasn't worth the loans. When the borrowers defaulted on their loans, the bank couldn't sell the collateral for enough to cover it. What happens if bitcoin drops to pennies? Then the bank's 'security' it took from MicroStrategy is worthless. Above is an example of leverage used for high-risk strategies. Not all leverage is high-risk, however. Some leverage can actually be used to reduce risk. This is what we call hedging, which we will cover at the end of the chapter.

NB – I want to stress that leveraging is not something that you should engage in as a novice. As long as you understand what leveraging is from the first few paragraphs, then there is no need to carry on with this chapter. Explaining leveraged financial instruments is very tricky, and although I have done my best to simplify it, not everyone I gave the content to understood it. If you are curious then read on. If you are struggling to understand it, then feel free to skip this chapter. This is by far one of the least important chapters in the book.

Leveraged ETFs

We have talked extensively about the multiple applications of ETFs. One of them being trackers for indexes such as the S&P 500 etc. For a normal index tracking ETF, when the index moves up by 1%, the ETF moves up by the same amount. For a leveraged ETF, depending on how leveraged it is, a 1% gain in the index can lead to a 3% gain in the ETF. This would be an ETF levered at 3:1. For a 2:1 leveraged ETF, for every 1% gain in the index we would see a 2% gain in the ETF. Of course, the converse is true if the index drops. If you wanted to bet on the index falling in price, you could buy an inverse ETF. This can be a 3:1 or 2:1, or even a 1:1 ratio, so if the index drops by 1%, the ETF increases by 1%. Even though the returns on an inverse 1:1 aren't amplified, it's still considered leveraged. We'll understand how when we learn about 'options' below. Apart from the risk of losing more money if the index goes against you, there is also the cost of leveraged ETFs that needs to be considered. The cost of owning a leveraged ETF is much more than the cost of none-leveraged index tracking ETFs. Management fees and transaction costs are both higher. So even if your leveraged ETF moves sideways and doesn't change price, you will still be losing money.

Options – Calls and Puts

An option is a contract, between two parties, enabling the owner of the option the ability to buy or sell the stock at a fixed price. This is known as the strike price. The option has an expiry date also, after which the contract becomes void if not acted upon. We will start with call options first. For a call option, the contract is to buy the asset at an agreed price. We would buy a call option if

40

we thought the price of the stock was going to increase. An option typically represents the right to buy shares at the fixed price, and the price one would pay is the price of the options contract. For example, your friend is selling pens for £1. You want to make a profit and you make an option contract to buy the pens at £1. Your plan is to wait for the pens to be valued at above £1, then buy 100 pens from your friend at the fixed £1 and sell them on at this higher price. You don't want to fork out £100 to buy the pens yet; you only want to buy them if the price goes above £1. Your friend agrees to sell you a call option to buy 100 pens at £1. He says he'll charge you £20 for the contract and that the offer to buy them at £1 will only last one month. To dissect the analogy, the strike price is £1 and the expiry is one month. The buyer of the theoretical 'call option' has the 'option' to buy 100 pens without having to actually buy all 100 pens. If the price of the pens doesn't go above £1, or becomes less than £1, he doesn't have to 'trigger' the contract and buy the 100 pens. He will just end up losing the £20 he gave his friend for the contract.

Let's apply this thinking to a real example. We think that Apple is going up after it published strong quarterly earnings. We want to buy a call option to profit from any bullish move (upward movement of a share price). The price of an Apple share price is $147. You buy a call option which has a strike price of $150 and an expiry date of two weeks. This means that at any point from now until the expiry date, you can buy a stock of Apple for $150. If in two weeks the price of Apple never goes above $150, then the call option expires and becomes worthless. If the price of Apple goes up to $155, then your call option is worth $5. As you could buy the share of Apple for $150 (as agreed upon in the option) and sell it immediately for $155, which is a $5 gain ($155-$150 = $5). So the total amount you make depends on the number of contracts you buy. If you bought 100 contracts, then you would make a $500 gain.

Nothing in life is free, and no one is going to let you buy a stock at a fixed price for free. The options contracts come with a cost. For the contract mentioned above, the cost is $1.85 per contract. This detracts from your profit of $5 of course. So per contract, what you make is $5.00-$1.85 = $3.15. As a call option represents 100 contracts (or 100 shares), this would mean the cost of the contract is $185 ($1.85 x 100), giving a profit of $315 ($3.15 x 100).

This is where the beauty of leverage comes in. If you had $185 in your pocket, you could do two things: buy an actual share of Apple, or leverage it and buy call options. If you were to do the former, then you can afford one share of Apple at $147. If it went up to $155, you would make a 5.44% profit. If instead you were to do the latter and buy an options contract with that $185, this would allow you to buy a call option representing 100 shares, and you would make a profit of 170% (as instead of profiting from only one share you can profit from 100 shares).

However, with great reward comes great risk. If the price of Apple doesn't reach more than $150 before it hits the expiry date, then the contract becomes void, and the $185 call options you bought are now worthless. This means you will have lost the whole $185. If you played it safe and bought the one share of Apple for $147, you'd still own an asset worth something (providing the share price doesn't drop to zero of course).

The option contract price varies on two factors. Firstly, how long is left until expiry, which makes sense as you have a longer time for the share price to move in your favour. And secondly, whether it is an 'in the money' or 'out of the money' option. A call option is classed as in the money if the value of the share is above the strike price. In the example above, the share has gone above the $147 price, to $155. This is an in the money call option. If we wanted to sell that option, then we would be selling an in the money call option, and the person would pay $5 per contract.

This is in the money, as the price of the share is above the strike price of $150. The out of the money call option is the one you bought originally, as the strike price of $150 was above the share price of $147. Call options are essentially betting on whether the stock will go up. If you're right you win big, and if you're wrong you lose it all.

Let's take a look at Puts. Unlike all the other financial instruments mentioned, Puts allow an investor to profit from a DECREASE in price. In the same way as a call option, there is a set strike price. The difference being at this price you have agreed to SELL the share, not buy it. You will only make money if you can sell the share at a higher price than you can buy it. If the market value drops below your strike price, your Put option goes up in value. Again, let's use another example to make things clearer. AMC's current market price is $15. For a Put with a strike price of $10.50, expiring in three weeks, the cost is $0.32. This means that if the share drops to $10.00 (within three weeks), you would make $0.18 per contract (drop in share price-cost of option $0.50-$0.32). If you invested $320 in Puts (buying 1,000 contracts, $0.32 x 1,000), you would make $180 in profit. If the share price dropped another $0.50 to $9.50, you would make $680 ($1.0-$0.32 x 1,000 contracts = $680).

If the mathematics is confusing don't worry! Just understand the concept that options allow you to use leveraging to bet on the stock price going up or down. You have the chance to make more and lose more than you would if you bought the actual stock, hence why it's a riskier investment.

Warrants

I don't want to delve too deeply into warrants, I just want you to know the difference between warrants and options.

A warrant, like an option, gives the holder the ability to buy a stock at a specified price and with a specified expiry date. The main difference between warrants and options is that warrants are issued by the company itself. Options on the other hand are issued by institutions or investors that own existing shares. To create a warrant, the company would have to create new shares, whereas for options they simply trade existing shares.

If a company you own is issuing warrants, then they are diluting how much of the company that us as shareholders own. They are reducing our shareholder equity. Think about it like this. When we buy a share, we own a proverbial piece of the pie, albeit a small one. When a company issues warrants, and they are triggered, then the new shares issued don't just materialise from thin air. They come from our pie, meaning that all the shareholders' slices get smaller, to make these new slices for the new shares issued. Conversely, there are also things management can do to make our slice bigger, but I'll leave that for Chapter 5.

NB – Warrants are often referred to as stock options, but bear in mind there is a slight difference.

Futures

Futures uses the same leveraging mechanism as options. The only difference is in the obligation to buy or sell. As indicated in the name, options give the holder the option of triggering the contract and buying or selling the shares. When the option expires, you can no longer buy or sell the shares attached to that option. For futures, the holder is obligated to buy or sell the shares at the fixed price on the expiry date. Thus, it never expires worthless like options, as the value of the futures contract would equal the value of the assets that the owner is obligated to buy.

Hedging

Everyone has heard of hedge funds, a very sexy term in the trading world. They are normally reserved for people of high net income, with a reputation for generating excellent returns. This reputation is most definitely over-inflated. Hedge funds charge very high fees, use riskier strategies and generate hugely varied returns. They normally perform much better during a bull market (when stocks are generally going up in price) vs a bear market (when stocks are generally dropping in price). In 2021 Melvin Capital, a major hedge fund, saw their portfolio drop by 41.5%, representing a loss of $7 billion. This didn't include the fees that clients had to pay for the performance.

The term hedging doesn't have much to do with the similar-sounding term hedge funds. Any investor can perform hedging as we will explain below. I'm sure you will have heard the expression, to 'hedge your bets.' If you haven't, it's basically a 'don't put all your eggs in one basket' approach. It ensures you are protected if things don't go to plan. Leveraging, although a risky tool, can be used in this way to decrease risk. For example, let's say that we think the price of gold is going to increase. We might then go out and buy gold mining stocks (companies that mine gold), which will increase in value should the price of gold rise. However, if the price of gold decreases, then our stocks will decrease in value.

If you wanted to hedge this bet, then you might want to buy something that will increase in price should the price of gold decrease. What we can buy is a put option on the gold price.[1] If the price of gold drops, we will lose money on our gold mining

---

1 For trading commodities like gold, we don't use options, we use futures contracts. In the case above, we would buy a futures contract which obliges us to sell gold at a fixed price, let's say £2,000. If the current price of gold falls below this fixed price, to £1,800, then we would make a profit. As we can by selling the gold for £2,000, which we are now able to buy for only £1,800.

shares but gain on our put option, offsetting our loss. Conversely, if the price of gold goes up, then our mining shares go up, but our put option becomes worthless. The point of hedging is that you put a small amount into your options, so if the trade goes in your stocks' favour you lose that small amount. If it goes against your stocks' favour, then that small amount you put into your options contracts will be amplified. This doesn't mean that it will mitigate completely the loss our shares will take, but it will definitely soften the blow. It's like buying home insurance – it's a small cost if you don't need it, but it pays out when things go wrong.

PART 2

COMPANY LOGISTICS

Chapter 5
Management

Management is an important, yet very overlooked, consideration for the investor. For a company, good leadership is essential for its ongoing success. As owners of a company, we want an excellent management team, who is focused on acting in the best interests of their shareholders. Even the most successful businesses have been ruined by bad management. I'll give you three examples of how bad management has prevailed.

1. **Failure to Innovate**

    Failure to Innovate – Toys 'R' Us. Depending on how old you are Toys 'R' Us really doesn't need any introduction. Its reputation as a toy store was unbeatable. If any analyst back then predicted the end of Toys 'R' Us they would have been ridiculed. For any Gen Zs reading this book, Toys 'R' Us was not only the go-to toy store, it was every kid's dream. Kids would beg their parents to go to Toys 'R' Us. It was like Hamleys in London; just much more accessible and actually affordable. Toys 'R' Us' management's problem was something called management myopia (myopia is a fancy word for short-sightedness). They were so comfortable being the centre of the toy world that they failed to innovate. The failure occurred around a time when other companies were embracing technology to attract the more online-savvy younger generations. Management's failure to adapt and move with the times turned a once thriving business into a case study.

2.   **Poor Asset Allocation**

Poor Asset Allocation – Lehman Brothers. Lehman Brothers were the fourth largest bank in the US, with 25,000 employees. They engaged heavily in subprime mortgages. When these mortgages collapsed, it caused the 2007–2008 financial meltdown. One of its most renowned culprits were the Lehman Brothers. They declared bankruptcy on 15 September, when the stock dropped by 93%.

3.   **Managerial Fraud**

Managerial Fraud – Enron. The Enron scandal hurt investors significantly. They did something they called 'creating accounting.' Andrew Fastow, who was promoted to CFO, developed a system to indicate the company was in good financial health. They hid their losses, debts and anything else they wanted to keep off the books. As a result, the share price was propped up, well above levels justified by the company's actual earnings. When this came to light, Enron's shares plummeted, falling to $0.26, from its peak of $90.75. Andrew Fastow was convicted of fraud and jailed for five years. Despite this, the shareholders still suffered the huge losses caused by irresponsible management.

These are but a few examples of poor management, the effect they can have on businesses, and the resultant knock-on effects felt by their shareholders. What we are going to look for are things that good management teams do. Ultimately, we want a management team that will act in the best interests of its shareholders. By 'in the best interests of its shareholders' I refer to any act that provides an increase in value to its shareholders. After all, the management team's wages are paid for by the owners.

Managerial Compensation

When the company pays wages and hands out bonuses to its employees, it is funded by its shareholders. Not directly in the sense that we have to fork out from our own pockets, but indirectly as they detract from the profit attributable to the shares we own. If the top executives at the company are given warrants (see Chapter 4) as bonuses, which is a common practice, then this detracts from our shareholder equity, as explained in the previous chapter.

The CEO is in charge of most of the goings-on of the company, apart from the pay of the top-level executives. This makes sense, as the CEO can't be the one deciding their own wage. This is decided by a board of directors, who are appointed by us, the shareholders. The board of directors are a group of people who represent the best interests of the shareholders, provide guidance to the CEO and general oversight of the company. One of the things the directors decide is the wages and bonuses that are paid to the executives of the company. The directors are supposed to be acting in the best interests of the shareholders, however, it is not unheard of for decisions to be affected by conflict of interests. The CEO and the directors may have familial or social relations which may affect the 'independent' directors' decision. The CEO has a role in deciding the compensation of the directors, while the directors decide the compensation of the CEO. You can see how an 'I scratch your back and you scratch my back' situation can very easily manifest itself with higher wages for all. Now, we may not be able to find out who is friends with whom; however, we can see how the pay of the CEO compares to other companies in a similar industry. We will learn in Part 3 how to assess a company's metrics to assess performance, and whether the management are delivering the growth of earnings that we might expect.

We need to ask ourselves, what have the management team done to deserve these wages and bonuses? What value have they brought to us shareholders? Are we able to justify the executive management's wages? Are the management spending our money wisely? In my view, bonuses should be given for excellent performance. The performance should be measured in a way that promotes long-term value increase. We will learn in Part 3 that "earnings" can be manipulated. If the CEO's bonus targets are based on earnings, then we are potentially encouraging what we refer to as 'creative' accounting, as that is the yardstick by which we are measuring the CEO.

Secondly, I believe that bonuses should be in the form of shares of the company, which CANNOT be sold by the receiver for a number of years. This means they can't just sell the shares straight after receiving them. The issuance and holding of the stock will help align the CEO's ideology with our own. Being a shareholder themselves, acting in the best interests of the shareholders is also beneficial to them.

In the Kodak scandal mentioned below, the company awarded the CEO options for 1.75 million shares of Kodak, the day before big news was due to be announced. The fact that the CEO was given this many shares the day before the big announcement was no coincidence. That announcement did in fact increase the value of the share by ten times. Despite the aforementioned problem of a management team diversifying into a completely unrelated area, it is also not a management team acting in the best interests of the shareholders.

The things we need to be looking at are whether the wages and bonuses paid are appropriate. Are they related to good performance, and do they encourage the executive to act in the shareholders' best interests?

Dividends

We went over what a dividend is when we covered equities in Chapter 1. If you have forgotten, please go back and give it another read. As a quick recap, dividends are payments a company makes to its shareholders, as a way of distributing its profits to its owners. They are normally expressed as a percentage (of the price of the share), and the company has no legal obligation to pay out dividends. Investing for dividends is a very legitimate tactic, but we will look more at investment stratagem in Part 4. The question we have to ask ourselves is, can we do a better job than the management team at creating value? Do we want the money paid out to invest as we please, or would we rather the management invest the money in the way they see fit? Most of you, including myself, when reading that statement in isolation will want the money paid out to us. But what if I told you that for the money to come to us, it gets taxed twice? The company pays corporation tax on its gross profit, then we pay dividend tax when it is paid into our bank account. If the company invest the money, they only pay corporation tax. If they are clever, they may even pay no tax, depending on how they choose to invest. Does this change your answer? I tell myself that if the management company is good, they can keep it, and if not, then I want my dividend. It then leads me to my next conundrum – if the management company isn't good, then why do I own their stock? The reason we might own a company with a questionable management team would be for speculation. In which case the speculator is looking for value via an increase in share price, not dividend payout. Making money via an increase in share price is called 'capital appreciation.' To break it down, the capital you own, in this case the share, has appreciated, or increased in value. If we use our rental property analogy, when you buy a property to rent (your stock), you make money in two ways: the rent money coming in (dividend) and the price of the property going up (capital appreciation).

Not all companies pay dividends, and unfortunately, it has become far too normalised not to pay a dividend. Many blue-chip stocks like Google (Alphabet) and Amazon gush cash, but elect not to pay out dividends. And why would they? The demand for stock is high, the share price is high and the public don't penalise them for not paying out. What us investors can excuse is companies with high growth. They don't pay dividends as they need the money to fund operations and support growth. The reason we invest in growth companies is for an increase in share price (capital appreciation), so I would prefer that they reinvest their profits into their own operations.

To summarise, management can either pay out to shareholders or invest the profits back into the company. The two ways investors can profit is via dividends or capital appreciation. If we choose to leave our money in management's hands, will they increase shareholder value?

Diversification

We mentioned the term diversification for investors when addressing ETFs and index funds in Chapter 4. We will readdress diversification for investors in Part 4 when we cover risk management. Companies themselves can also diversify into different sectors. Amazon, as an example, generates a profit, then reinvests this profit by entering a new sector. It then generates more income and continues to grow. An example of a new sector it entered is the entertainment industry – Prime Video. This encourages more people to sign up to the Amazon Prime subscription, so Amazon makes more money. Your stock as a result makes more profit, and your stock price, which is based on Amazon's potential earnings, goes up. This means your asset (the stock you own) has appreciated in value.

Above is an example where a company diversifies and expands into new industries, to grow profits and ultimately increase the price of shares. When a company has good management, which make good management decisions, I am happy for them to not pay out a dividend. Even if they invest their profits buying the exact same shares I do, they will make more for the shareholders due to the tax saving mentioned earlier. It's worth noting that tax doesn't escape us completely by not receiving dividends. If we ever choose to sell the stock and capture the profits, we have to pay capital gains tax (only if we make a profit selling of course). This, however, can be avoided through tax saving schemes which we will cover in Chapter 16.

As investors we always like companies that are continually looking to grow and expand their operations. Lack of growth and innovation from management will lead to stagnation or decline in revenue. As we saw above for Toys 'R' Us, lack of innovation can be catastrophic for investors.

Mergers and Acquisitions (M&A)

The easiest way to describe mergers and acquisitions is as the expansion of a company by buying over (acquiring) or joining another company (merging). We have to appreciate that there is a finite amount of money that can be made in one industry. The growth of businesses is similar to population growth. They have a period of slower growth, then fast growth, then slower growth. See Figure 5:1 outlining business lifecycle. A market does have a saturation point, at which time it may be more efficient to expand into a different market. The caveat being that management are good decision-makers. If done well, they can really profit from acquisitions. Below, I'll include examples of questionable and excellent decision making.

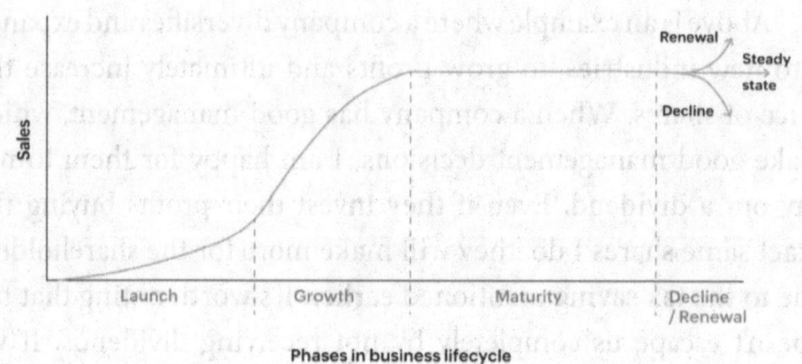

Figure 5:1: Business Lifecycle.

Questionable decision making happens when an adventurous management team and lots of free cash come together. Management get twitchy and decide to acquire another company, in a sector that has nothing to do with the company they are part of. One example is Kodak. They are a camera company who in 1988 decide to acquire Sterling pharmaceutical company for £5.1 billion. What business does a camera company have running a pharmaceutical company! Shock, they ended up selling the company they acquired for less than they bought it. What's even more ludicrous is that Trump was willing to give Kodak $765 million from the emergency fund reserve during peak COVID times to establish a pharmaceutical business. The US government wanted to give a camera company, who had tried and failed before, $765 million to start selling medicines. Thankfully, they didn't end up getting the money in the end due to managerial fraud (discussed below), but the fact that they almost got the money still baffles me. Another example is AMC. This is a cinema company that was revived from the dead by Reddit, otherwise known as a 'meme' stock. They recently purchased 22% of Hycroft Mining

56

Holding Corporation for $27.9 million. This is a mine which was non-operational, as the cost of extracting the gold cost more than what they were able to sell it for (the price of gold). What we might be asking ourselves is, what does the management of the cinema industry know about gold mining? How have they taken it upon themselves to spend $27.9 million of shareholder equity on a non-operational gold mine? Even if they are right, and the price of gold rockets, can we really call this a sensible management team? In their defence, you could say that the cinema industry is a dying industry, especially with the emergence of Netflix etc. So AMC were just trying to diversify. I agree with sensible diversification, but gold mining is an industry residing in a different galaxy to the industry that AMC management team has been operating in. Of all the gold mines to choose from, Hycroft Mining was a questionable decision nonetheless.

Ask yourself, is this the kind of management team you want keeping your profits? Or would you rather they pay you your profits as dividends so you can reinvest them as you wish? It may turn out that you want to invest that dividend into a speculative mining company, but that should be your choice, not one made for you by an irresponsible management team.

On the flip side, one of the best acquirers is none other than Coca-Cola. They have acquired so many drinks brands that you would never have known. They own 200 brands worldwide. In the UK for example, they do not only own other fizzy drinks like Fanta and Sprite, but sports drinks like Powerade, a water brand called Smartwater and even Costa Coffee! This is an example of a company sticking to a sector in which they are undoubtedly experts. If anyone knows how to identify a good drink, or how to market and sell a drink, it's the owners of the most addictive drink out there, Coke. Coca-Cola's management team has delivered great company growth, expanding in the sector they know best. Everything for them takes less effort, as the infrastructure required to produce drinks is already in place. In this way they benefit from something called 'economy of size.' Their size means things cost less as they already have the machinery needed to make the drinks. They also have bargaining power with the suppliers they use for their ingredients, as they order in such large quantities. Let's explain this with an example. Imagine we are the business that provides plastic bottles to Coca-Cola. We live in an inflationary world right now (Part 3), so our prices are going up. We push these prices onto Coca-Cola and ask them to pay more per bottle. If they refuse to pay more, we can't risk telling them to take their business elsewhere. They are a big customer for us, so the risk of losing them to a competitor is too great. In this sense they have pricing power. This is the same way that Walmart manage to keep their prices so low; the suppliers are the ones that 'pay the price.'

Coca-Cola has a management team that has behaved responsibly, has allocated shareholder capital effectively and has sustained consistent growth for its owners. None other than the legendary investor Warren Buffett is a big believer and large shareholder in the business.

Share Repurchases

Share repurchases (or share buybacks) is when a company buys up its own shares. By doing so they reduce the number of shares in existence, giving their shareholders a bigger piece of the pie. Look at it like this. A company makes £300,000 and is made up of three shares. Each share gets a third of the profits – £100,000. If the company was to repurchase one of the shares, then there would only be two shares in existence. Each share would now be entitled to £150,000. In this way, each share is now worth more. By decreasing the number of shares, the existing shares become entitled to more, and hence become more valuable. Share repurchases increase a share's earning per share, or EPS as it's known. The company is in effect buying more of its own shares on your behalf. Now you do not actually receive more shares, your share is just worth more. From the above example, you can appreciate how a share that makes £100k profit is far less valuable than one that makes £150k.

The main considerations for share buybacks comprise of two questions. The first being, how many new shares are being issued?

New shares can be issued to raise more capital, for the exact same reason that they were issued in the first place (see Chapter 1). Or they can be issued as warrants for managerial compensation. For those that didn't read the chapter on leveraging, warrants are permissions to buy shares at a certain price. The shares are newly issued, therefore increase the number of existing shares the company has.

If the company increases the number of shares by, let's say, 1,000 shares, and buys backs only 500 shares, then we are worse off as an equity holder. Our equity has decreased by whatever percentage the new 500 shares issued makes of the total number of outstanding shares. If the company buys back 1,000 shares, it just cancels out the ones it issued. It may seem like an excellent repurchase, when in actual fact it leaves the shareholder no better off.

The second question to ask is, what price are the companies paying for their shares? Many companies make repurchases at the worst time. They will repurchase their shares when the stock price is high, and not when the stock price is low. The reason they do this must align with the mentality of buying shares when they are 'on the up.' However, this goes against all logic. When acquiring an asset, you want to get it at the lowest possible price.

One reason for purchases made at the wrong price comes down to benefiting the companies' executives. As discussed above, they often receive their compensation via the issuance of new stock. Buybacks serve to counter the new shares issued to them, as well as increase the earnings per share (EPS) and hence the share price. They then can offload the stock they were given and make a handsome profit, even when the money could have been spent in the shareholders' best interests. Take the company The Home Depot. The CEO, Craig Menear, and his team announced plans to buy back $4 billion worth of shares. This news prompted an increase in share prices, to which Menear responded by selling 113,687 shares, pocketing $18 million. The next day he was given 38,689 newly issued shares, of which he shortly afterwards sold another 63%, to make a further $4.5 million. His actions should beg the question, is this team acting in the best interests of the shareholders? Are they deploying our cash in a way that is most effective for us or for their own gain?

A less sinister reason for poorly timed share repurchases has to do with excess cash reserves. If a company has a good year and generates more profits, it will also have more cash to deploy. By virtue of its strong earnings for the year, its stock price will increase in value. Hence the shares are repurchased at higher prices. Similarly, for years of underperformance, even though the shares are selling at a discounted price, the company may have less cash, thus choose to be more frugal with its repurchases.

All in all, it comes down to how well a management team leads the company and how it allocates shareholder capital. A good management team is one that is driven to produce positive revenue growth, acts in the best interests of its owners, makes good decisions and ultimately increases shareholder equity.

Chapter 6
Financial Statements

While we may not strive to be accountants, I think a basic understanding of financial reporting is important for any investor. Financial reports can give us both qualitative and quantitative information about the company. Reports are released quarterly (every three months), labelled Q1–Q4, with an annual report summarising the year's performance. Within each report, we can find management's comments on the performance of the company, any setbacks, projected future earnings etc. The reports also contain the financial statements, which quantitively inform us about the company's current earnings, efficiency and its financial health. We will go through some of the qualitative things we might want to know before diving into the quantitative analysis.

There is a bit of maths in this section, so don't worry if you struggle to understand everything. A general understanding of the underlying concepts will more than suffice.

Qualitative

Looking at the non-numerical data allows us to conduct a qualitative analysis of a stock. It gives us reasons to invest in a stock based on the type of business, quality of product, branding power etc. Reading the financial reports can give you a lot of information about how the business runs, which is important to know if it's a company you want to buy. To make this more tangible, it may be worth flipping over to Chapter 17 to read only the qualitative analysis sections for the case studies discussed. This will give you an idea of what we look for when buying a share.

The best way to learn about financial reports is to dive straight into the deep end and look at a real financial statement. The example I am going to pick is Build-A-Bear, a company I'm sure many of you with children, nieces and nephews have heard of. For those of you that haven't, it's a store where you can customise, build your own bear and see it being fabricated. I decided to pick this company as its qualitative earnings call was what prompted me to sell the company. The first thing on every report is the contents. It is a good way to navigate it unless you want to read the whole thing.

PART I

Let's start with Part I. Item 1 tells you about exactly what the business does, a description of its operations and its strategies for maximising earnings. For example, they talk about increasing lifetime value of customers by bringing in a 'Build-A-Bear Bonus Club' loyalty programme. About 'real estate portfolio diversification', opening up shops in malls, cruise ships and seasonal pop-up shops to reach a broader customer base. It even has a section about its competition in the stuffed animal business, mentioning other brands like Hasbro, Ty etc.

Item 1A discusses risk factors, explaining things that can affect the business' profitability. It mentions COVID and the impact of reduced foot traffic at malls (where a lot of their stall are situated). It also talks about supply chain issues. It states that because they only have four vendors, should there be any delays or increase in supply costs, finding a new supplier may not be possible in a timely manner, causing delays and affecting earnings. It mentions that the suppliers are all foreign, increasing the risk of importation problems etc. It even talks about how fluctuations in its quarterly earnings may result in a decline in its stock price. This is a great section to read, as it gives you factors that could impact the company negatively, which will in turn effect our decision to buy the stock.

Item 2 has a section on property, stating that it leases all of its store locations. It does, however, own a warehouse and a distribution centre. As investors buying this stock, it's important we don't attribute the 372 retail stores to their asset column, as they don't own the buildings, only the leases. The next thing I would like to know is how long their leases are. If they are short-term leases, subject to price increases, then this will eat the profits if this is the case for all 372 stores. If they are long leases, then this is much better for the investor. This is very different to McDonald's, which owns most of its stores. The founder of McDonald's, Ray Kroc, went to an MBA class and asked a student: "What business is McDonald's in?". The student, dumbfounded, looked at him and said, "The food industry." He laughed and said, "No, we're in the real estate business." As an investor you wouldn't know this unless you read the financial report.

Items 3 and 4 refer to legal or health and safety issues, which are always good to check, as some lawsuits can be enough to put a dent in the company's coffers. Take the Apple and Samsung lawsuit, which resulted in a $1.049 billion payout from Samsung to Apple.

PART II

Part II contains most of the 'numbers' and information about the earnings of the company. Item 5 talks about the share repurchase programme, detailing the number of shares and the average price they repurchased at. Both showing the size/significance of the repurchases and also whether the shares were brought at reasonable prices (see Chapter 5). Item 7 contains a more in-depth discussion about the business' performance and comments on its financial health, including talking about its debt, its cash reserves, income tax etc. Item 8 contains the main elements of the financial statement, where we can find the revenue, costs, income and other useful data (we will cover financial statements below). The full financial statement is usually tacked onto the end of the document and can be seen in Part IV. Item 9 contains a spiel about the auditing of their financial statement, and how it is officially signed off by an accountancy firm as a seal of legitimacy. This is something that is required to be listed on the major stock exchanges as a publicly traded company. The style of accounting most commonly used is called 'GAAP'. Like all accounting systems, this form of accounting has its pros and cons; however, we will not delve too deeply into this as we don't want to send you to sleep.

PART III

This is where they mention the management team. They usually discuss their accolades and why they are fit for the job. For example, the CEO's résumé includes their previous experience of toy companies such as Hasbro, Checkerboard Toys, Mattel and others. In Item 11 and 12 they mention executive compensation, which, as discussed in Chapter 5, is how much the management receive in wages, warrants and bonuses.

The image below details the number of shares issued that year, plus the price they were issued at. We talked about options and warrants in Chapters 4 and 5. What we need to note is the price they were sold at compared to the current market price. The price they were sold at is $9.76 per share. If the share price of Build-A-Bear was $11, then management are buying them at a huge discount. It will be the shareholders who pay for this. As it happens, the share price at the time was less than $9.76. This serves as a good incentive for the management team to increase the share price of the stock, as the options at a strike price of

$9.76 are only worth something if the share price goes above $9.76. This is an important section to look at. If the management are receiving excessive compensation, and delivering mediocre results, what's their incentive to do better for the shareholders? And why are we paying their bonuses if they aren't creating value for us, their owners?

Plan category	(a) Number of securities to be issued upon exercise of outstanding options, warrants and rights	(b) Weighted-average exercise price of outstanding options, warrants and rights
Equity compensation plans approved by security holders	923,254	$9.76
Total	923,254	$9.76

Figure 6:2: Build-A-Bear Shares Issued.

This is an example of one annual report. Bear in mind the structure can change from company to company, though the general gist is the same. As you can see, it gives us a lot of information about the company. Importantly, it gives us the management's outlook and plans for the company, which is essential to know as owners. If you ran a shop, would you not oversee your managers? Of course you would! So there is no reason not to do the same for any shares you buy. In the next sections we will delve more into the numbers, go over the composition of a balance sheet and explain the contents of earnings statements.

Balance Sheets

A balance sheet, in simplified terms, is a report that tells us what a company has to its name. It contains two columns, assets and liabilities. They MUST balance at the end, hence the name 'balance' sheets. So what do these two terms mean? An asset is an item owned by a company that holds value. This item can be something physical like cash or property, or it can be something intangible, like goodwill (covered below).

Liabilities refer to the obligations of a company to another entity. In simplified terms, what the company owes other people. These obligations result in 'future sacrifices of economic benefit.' The obvious examples are loans and debts, which represent a future 'sacrifice' to pay these off. The other category that comes under this banner is equity. Equity refers to the part of the company that the shareholders own. This would come under the liabilities section but is more of a separate entity. If it's getting a bit overwhelming then don't worry, we are going to systematically go through Build-A-Bear's balance sheet together.

	February 1, 2020
ASSETS (Dollars in thousands, except share data)	
Current assets:	
Cash and cash equivalents	$ 26,726
Inventories, net	53,381
Receivables, net	11,526
Prepaid expenses and other current assets	7,117
Total current assets	98,750

Figure 6:3: Build-A-Bear Balance Sheet – Current Assets.

The first thing to note with any financial report are the brackets at the top, just below the heading (see Figure 6:3). It tells us the currency and amounts that we are dealing with. It says 'dollars in thousands,' so everything in the columns needs to be multiplied by 1,000. As we will see in the Apple balance sheet later, is has a similar line, apart from the 'small' distinction that it says 'dollars in millions.' Note that it states 'except share data,' which is found in most financial reports. In Figure 6:3 we have the first half of the balance sheet, the assets column. In other words what the company owns.

The first half of the asset column is the company's current assets. These refer to assets that can be converted into cash in a short time frame, usually under a year.

1. **Cash and cash equivalents.**
   These are obviously the most liquid of the company's assets. It's always good to see a company with a good cash reserve, as if they fall into difficulties, cash reserves that can be deployed quickly are crucial.
2. **Inventories.**
   This refers to the value of the stock cupboard, or the unsold items that a company has. If a company is not performing and struggling to sell its items, then you may see the inventory increase. Even some of the top companies can see inventory increases. Nike, for example, in 2022, saw a 44% increase in inventory vs the previous year. In Nike's case, this is most likely due to reduced consumer spending due to a recessionary environment (see Chapter 7). When products are struggling to sell because they go 'out of fashion,' you can also expect an increase in inventory. A sustained increase in inventory year over year is something to look out for.
3. **Receivables.**
   This is money owed to the company for services rendered which has not yet been paid.

4. **Prepaid expenses**

    Prepad expenses are things that have been paid for in advance, and hence represent value. For example, if you buy a yearly Amazon Prime subscription, you get twelve months of free delivery. This gives the company a value, as if you bought the company and its assets, you would also get this twelve-month subscription. This is an asset that needs to be 'written down.' This means that one month later you only have eleven months of subscription, so your prepaid expenses are only worth eleven months of subscription. In this way some assets are reduced to zero as they are used.

5. **Other current assets**

    In the section below the balance sheet there is text which provides commentary on the items above. The annual report may or may not give more information on what these 'other' current assets are.

For non-current assets, we have items that cannot be easily converted into cash. They are usually displayed directly below the current assets table. See Figure 6:4.

Operating lease right-of-use asset	104,825
Property and equipment, net	52,973
Deferred tax assets	
Other assets, net	3,381
Total Assets	**$ 261,372**

Figure 6:4: Build-A-Bear Balance Sheet – Non-Current Assets.

These include:

1. **Operating lease right-of-use asset.**

    As we learnt from the qualitative section, Build-A-Bear leases almost all its property. It has valued the ownership of these leases at $126 million. How it comes to this value is very much up for debate. It is an estimated or made-up figure, if you will.

2. **Property and equipment.**

    As we know from Part I, the property refers to the warehouse and distribution centre they own, and the equipment will be the machines they have in stores to make the bears etc.

3. **Deferred tax assets.**

    This item is included on a balance sheet when a company has overpaid their tax bill for the year. Although they don't have the cash in hand, this excess of tax paid does have a quantifiable value. An analogy is like paying your rent in advance.[1]

4. **Intangible assets.**

    The word intangible means something that doesn't have a physical presence. A common intangible asset on the balance sheet is goodwill. Goodwill is the part of a company's value that can't be quantified. It refers to a company's good reputation or brand loyalty. I would not say Build-A-Bear has a particularly noteworthy brand loyalty, hence that space is blank. Apple on the other hand has huge brand loyalty, with an almost cult-like following. Here we would expect to see a figure on the balance sheet.

5. **Other assets**

    Other assets can be many things. On scrolling further down you will find an explanation for what this refers to. One of

---

1 When looking through balance sheets you may also see deferred tax liability, which is the opposite of a deferred tax asset

the items it refers to in Build-A-Bear's case is the costs for a film they released. They describe it as 'capitalizable direct costs, production overhead…'. If the film is a flop and doesn't lead to any increase in sales, then one could say this is more of a liability than an asset. However, here it is listed as an asset.

Before we have a look at the asset sheet for Apple, let's talk about why we might want to look at a company's assets. When we buy a company, we want to see what we are buying. The larger the company's assets, the higher its value, as if you own the share you also have a claim to those assets. If Build-A-Bear owned the stores instead of leasing them its asset value would increase dramatically. As we have seen, they put a figure of $126 million on the value of their leases. This has to be looked at with some scrutiny, as it is unlikely that they can sell their leases to a third party and raise anything like $126 million. Some companies can be creative with their accounting and can heavily inflate their assets. The leases or the film production costs are examples of exaggeration. Another way a company can 'increase' the value of their assets is by giving intangible assets like goodwill a higher value than is appropriate.

We have established that the shareholder has a claim to the assets. However, when will this manifest into anything tangible for its shareholders? In times of bankruptcy, the assets are sold and divided among its debtors and shareholders. First of all, the debtors are the first ones to be paid off. Bear in mind these debtors include bondholders (see Chapter 2). We will look at all of this when we come to the liabilities section below. The shareholders are only paid in a bankruptcy, if the value of assets are greater than the value of the debt. What is left over after paying off all the debts is what belongs to the shareholders. We need to be wary of what has been included in the non-current asset column when assessing this. If a company has a large value attributed to goodwill, then this has no value for a company going bankrupt and thus should not be included in any calculations. Often you will see book value quoted. This is what is used to estimate what a company is worth on its 'books' to its shareholders. This is an invariably overstated figure, of which only a fraction will be realised by shareholders should a company go bankrupt. We will cover the calculations of book value in more depth in Chapter 10. Benjamin Graham, the godfather of investing, recommended using just the current asset value (minus the liabilities) to calculate what a shareholder would receive from liquidation (selling of assets in bankruptcy) of a company.

The second thing we look for is how financially healthy a company is. Does it have large cash holdings, or a high value of current assets compared to its debt? If a company's debts are much larger than its assets, then we have to assess the company's ability to pay back its debts and the risk of it defaulting and declaring bankruptcy.

Before we go into liabilities, let's have a look at the asset columns for Apple below in Figure 6:5.

ASSETS: (In millions, except number of shares)	September 24, 2022	September 25, 2021
Current assets:		
Cash and cash equivalents	$ 23,646	$ 34,940
Marketable securities	24,658	27,699
Accounts receivable, net	28,184	26,278
Inventories	4,946	6,580
Vendor non-trade receivables	32,748	25,228
Other current assets	21,223	14,111
Total current assets	135,405	134,836
Non-current assets:		
Marketable securities	120,805	127,877
Property, plant and equipment, net	42,117	39,440
Other non-current assets	54,428	48,849
Total non-current assets	217,350	216,166
Total assets	$ 352,755	$ 351,002

Figure 6:5: Apple – Balance Sheet – Asset Columns (in millions).

This balance sheet shows two years of data, which allows us to assess change. To properly assess a company's trajectory or trend, one should look back further than two years. There are websites like Morningstar or Macrotrends, where a company's entire financial history is laid out for ease of comparison.

An item on Apple's balance sheet that was not on Build-A-Bear's balance sheet is marketable securities. These refer to the same securities we discussed in Chapters 1 and 2, which may be stocks or bonds. You may have noticed that this item appears both in the current and non-current sections. The reason being, that some securities have a certain time after which the money invested cannot be withdrawn. Government bonds are a good example of this. The marketable securities in the non-current portion refers to money tied in for more than a year, whereas the items listed in the current asset section can be equities or bonds with no or short 'tie-in'.

TASK – Take a look at Figure 6:5, and see if you can remember what each line means. Look back to earlier when we talked about Figure 6:3 and 6:4 if you have forgotten.

Liabilities

Liabilities are defined as something a person or a company owes. These can include debts, mortgages, accounts payable, expenses, bonds etc. See them as the opposite of assets. They, like assets, have current and non-current sections. This is also based on the timeline of when the debtor is owed. Let's look at Apple's liability column below.

Current liabilities:			
Accounts payable	$	64,115	$ 54,763
Other current liabilities		60,845	47,493
Deferred revenue		7,912	7,612
Commercial paper		9,982	6,000
Term debt		11,128	9,613
Total current liabilities		153,982	125,481
Non-current liabilities:			
Term debt		98,959	109,106
Other non-current liabilities		49,142	53,325
Total non-current liabilities		148,101	162,431
Total liabilities		302,083	287,912

Figure 6:6: Apple – Liability Column (in millions).

Before we comment on Apple's liabilities, let's explain some of the terms which are not obvious from Figure 6:6:

1. **Accounts payable**
   The company's obligation to creditors or suppliers that have not been paid.
2. **Deferred revenue**
   Payments received from the company's customers for a service or item that has not yet been delivered.
3. **Commercial paper**
   A short-term loan which is issued for a company to finance their short-term liabilities, such as accounts payable etc.

We need to bear in mind that we are not considering simply the size of liabilities, but their relative size when compared to a company's assets and earnings. One thing we want to look for is something called working capital. It's a gauge to measure a company's short-term health. The way to calculate this is by subtracting current liabilities from current assets.

Working capital = Current assets – Current liabilities

If a company has a significant large working capital, it suggests they have good short-term financial health and good liquidity. This is a desirable, as it means the company has money to invest in the business to generate growth. However, it may be worth looking at why this is. If the large working capital is down to a large and increasing inventory, then we need to ask why is the inventory being stockpiled and isn't selling?

If the working capital is negative, then that suggests that the company's short-term financial health may not be ideal. This is where we need to consider the earning power of these companies. If they have earnings that easily cover their short-term obligations/debts, then a negative working capital may not be a concern. If their earnings don't cover the short-term debt comfortably, then this may be cause for concern.

TASK – Take a few minutes and see if you can calculate Apple's working capital from Figures 6:5 and 6:6 (use the 2022 column from Figure 6:5).

Let's go through it:

Apples's Working Cap = Apple's Current assets – Apple's Current Liabilities

Apple's Working cap (Figures in Millions) = $135,405 – $153,982 = $18,577

In the case of Apple, they have a negative working cap of $18.5 billion (remember that figures for Apple's balance sheet are expressed in millions). This is no small figure, and not something we might have expected from a company as successful as Apple.

We now need to think about their earning power. Do they

have earnings that can easily cover their short-term liabilities? Apple have very predictable and high earnings, as we will see when we look at their income statement. Apple can thus afford to have a negative working cap of such a size. Their maintenance of a negative working cap is indicative of their own confidence in their position.

For companies with negative working caps, we need to question how they will be able to pay off their debts. If not from the earnings then the only two options are to take on more debt, or to declare bankruptcy.

When analysing a company's financial statements, you will see many different metrics, which are normally expressed as ratios. The reason ratios are used is because the raw figure on its own doesn't paint the full picture. The current assets and cash mean nothing if we don't know how high the company's debts are. As they can't use cash to increase shareholder value if it's owed to another party.

Two ratios you may come across which compare assets and liabilities are the current ratio and the quick ratio. The current ratio is calculated using the same figures as working cap calculation, but we divide the figures instead of subtracting them.

$$Current\ ratio = \frac{Current\ assets}{Current\ Liabilities}$$

The quick ratio is a stricter measure of company health and only takes the items from the current assets that are quickly converted to cash. These being cash and cash equivalents, marketable securities and accounts receivable. We then proceed in the same way as above.

$$Quick\ ratio = \frac{Current\ assets\ most\ readily\ liquidated}{Current\ liabilities}$$

I don't have a hard-and-fast rule with regards to the minimum current and quick ratios I need to invest. As discussed above, it really depends on the earnings of the company. As a general rule, I like to see a current ratio of greater than 1.75 and a quick ratio higher than 0.5. However, this is not an absolute; some of my higher-risk investments don't meet this criteria. While it may seem that the higher the ratio the better, if the quick ratio is too high, it may suggest that the company is not deploying its assets and cash effectively to generate growth for the company.

Shareholder Equity

Shareholder equity is what is left over of the assets after the liabilities have been accounted for. These are assets available to shareholders, the equity left when all the debtors have been paid. When we talked about book value earlier, it is the same as this number. To recap:

Shareholder equity or book value = total assets – total liabilities

To dissect the shareholder equity statement, the top line is the **Total shareholders' equity** at the start of the recording period. This tells us the amount of equity attributable to the shareholders, which can be calculated from the equation above.

The rest of the statement covers changes to the shareholder equity. In other words, changes to the value attributed to the shares. **Net income** is the income after expenses and tax. We will look at this below when we cover income statements. In the **Dividends and dividend equivalents** row, you will see that the amounts are in brackets. When an amount is in brackets it means it's a negative number. This makes sense as dividends paid out to shareholders detract from money attributable to the shares. It shouldn't necessarily be seen as a loss, as the money is moving from belonging to the shares to belonging to the owner of the shares. The only thing to consider is the dividend tax that it accrues, but we will cover this in Chapter 16. At the bottom of the table we can see the **Dividends declared per share**. For Apple we can see that they have increased the dividends paid out three years in a row by an average of 6.3% year over year. A dividend growing year over year is always a good sign, provided the dividend payment is sustainable. Given the ratio of the net income against the dividend, it's safe to say that Apple's dividend is most certainly sustainable.

	September 24, 2022	September 25, 2021	September 26, 2020
Total shareholders' equity, beginning balances	$ 63,090	$ 65,339	$ 90,488
Common stock and additional paid-in capital:			
Beginning balances	57,365	50,779	45,174
Common stock issued	1,175	1,105	880
Common stock withheld related to net share settlement of equity awards	(2,971)	(2,627)	(2,250)
Share-based compensation	9,280	8,108	6,975
Ending balances	64,849	57,365	50,779
Retained earnings/(Accumulated deficit):			
Beginning balances	5,562	14,966	45,898
Net income	99,803	94,680	57,411
Dividends and dividend equivalents declared	(14,793)	(14,431)	(14,087)
Common stock withheld related to net share settlement of equity awards	(3,454)	(4,151)	(1,604)
Common stock repurchased	(90,186)	(85,502)	(72,516)
Cumulative effect of change in accounting principle			(136)
Ending balances	(3,068)	5,562	14,966
Accumulated other comprehensive income/(loss)			
Beginning balances	163	(406)	(584)
Other comprehensive income/(loss)	(11,272)	569	42
Cumulative effect of change in accounting principle			136
Ending balances	(11,109)	163	(406)
Total shareholders' equity, ending balances	$ 50,672	$ 63,090	$ 65,339
Dividends and dividend equivalents declared per share or RSU	$ 0.90	$ 0.85	$ 0.795

Figure 6:7: Apple – Total Shareholder's Equity.

The other item of note is the **Common stock repurchased** row. Apple repurchased $90 billion dollars of Apple stock. We discussed stock repurchases In Chapter 5. To recap, repurchasing stock is like a company buying back their own stock on the shareholders' behalf. So it increases the equity per share. They could pay this out as dividend, allowing us to invest the money as we choose, or invest it back into the business to generate growth. The question we have to ask is, do we want the company to buy more stock on our behalf? Are they spending our money in the most effective way?

The rest of the section involves other causes of equity loss, ending with a balance of around $50 million. This amount is less compared to the other years, in part due to the large stock repurchase programmes.

TASK – Look through the balance sheets of Microsoft. See if you can see any similarities or make any observations like the ones we discussed.

I know most of you will keep on reading without doing the task, but the best way to learn is to apply the knowledge! So please don't skip this step, it will be invaluable if you want to learn to do a deeper dive into your future investments.

Income Statements

We now understand what a balance sheet comprises of, and the importance of evaluating the health of a company and the other aspects such as dividends and share repurchases. The next thing we need to look at is how much money the business is bringing in, and how efficiently it does so. We also need to see whether the income is stable, increasing or decreasing compared to previous years.

The first line is **Net sales**. Net in this sense is slightly misleading, but consider this number as the total amount of money paid into the business from all its product sales. They have split sales into products and services. The former being all the gadgets it sells and the latter being subscription services like AppleCare, cloud storage etc. We can compare this figure to the previous years, and see if there is a trend in sales. In Apple's case, they increased year on year for the last three years.

The next thing to note is what it costs Apple to make these sales, and how much profit they make on their sales. We can see the cost broken down into cost of sales and operating expenses. Both need to be taken into account when calculating Apple's profit margin. The **Total cost of sales** is $223,546 million and the **Total operating expenses** is $51,345 million. Together the expenses come to $274,891 million (223,546 + 51,345 = 274,891).

	September 24, 2022	September 25, 2021	September 26, 2020
Net sales:			
Products	$ 316,199	$ 297,392	$ 220,747
Services	78,129	68,425	53,768
Total net sales	394,328	365,817	274,515
Cost of sales:			
Products	201,471	192,266	151,286
Services	22,075	20,715	18,273
Total cost of sales	223,546	212,981	169,559
Gross margin	170,782	152,836	104,956
Operating expenses:			
Research and development	26,251	21,914	18,752
Selling, general and administrative	25,094	21,973	19,916
Total operating expenses	51,345	43,887	38,668

Figure 6:8: Apple – Sales.

The one item worth commenting on is **Research and development** (known as R&D), which comes under operating expenses. To keep their products and technology relevant, Apple needs to spend money on innovating and exploring new products. If you remember the example of Toys 'R' Us in the chapter on management, their failure to innovate and implement technology was a major reason for their downfall. The money Apple spend on R&D will help them maintain the sales growth they have enjoyed for the three years listed above. We also have to bear in mind that R&D is tax deductible. If it leads to an increase in sales then it may also increase shareholder dividend payments, and even an increase share price. If done well, money spent on R&D is money well spent. In start-ups, R&D will be a big part of the budget, as they will be spending money on developing their product.

Operating income	119,437	108,949	66,288
Other income/(expense), net	(334)	258	803
Income before provision for income taxes	119,103	109,207	67,091
Provision for income taxes	19,300	14,527	9,680
Net income	$ 99,803	$ 94,680	$ 57,411

Figure 6:9: Apple – Gross and Net Income.

The last part of the income statement is the gross and net income. Gross income is the total sales minus all the expenses that come from the generating the sales.

Gross income - Total Sales – Total Expenses

To calculate this it would be the Sales figure of $394,328 – total expenses figure of $274,891 (which we calculated above). This would give us a gross income of $119,437 million.

Gross Income (In Millions) = $394,328 – $274,891 = $119,437

If you look at the first line in Figure 6:9, **Operating income** is the same number as we calculated above. Gross income and operating income are synonymous (though **Gross margin** which you may have spotted in the Figure 6:8 is slightly different).

The **Net income** is the figure you get when you deduct the tax bill from the **Operating/Gross income**. It is effectively the money left in the company's pocket after everyone else has been paid. You will see the **Provision for income taxes** and some other expenses deducted (not put in brackets for some reason) to give us the final net income of $99,803 million.

It is useful to evaluate how efficiently the business is run. The operating profit margin (OPM) tells us how much it costs a company to generate its sales. An efficiently run company keeps its costs to a minimum, to maximise its OPM. To calculate this, we divide the gross income (or operating income) by the net sales.

$$Operating\ Profit\ Margin\ (OPM) = \frac{Gross\ income}{Net\ sales}$$

If we want to calculate net profit margin, we would use net income instead of gross income. This may be a better measure if you are comparing businesses in different countries which pay different rates of tax.

$$Net\ Profit\ Margin = \frac{Net\ income}{Net\ sales}$$

Simply put, the profit margin looks at what portion of the **Net sales** the company keeps. For Apple, this comes to:

$$Operating\ Profit\ Margin\ (OPM) = \frac{\$119,437}{\$394,328} \times 100 = 30\%$$

For an OPM, this is excellent. Technology stocks often enjoy

82

healthy OPMs as they have low running costs. The main cost comes from developing the software. Compare this to mining companies. They have much higher costs such as the land, machinery, energy and manpower. To give an example, one of the biggest gold miners in the world, Harmony Gold Mining, have a negative OPM! Their 2022 sales amount to $42,645 million. Their expenses on the other hand come to $43,157 million. Another company we looked at was Build-A-Bear. Their OPM is 9.5%, which is a big difference to Apple's 30%. This is one of the reasons why technology stocks are so hot, as they have higher OPMs than other industries.

While looking at the company's earnings is important, checking the company's cash flow is prudent. Earnings can be manipulated. What is called creative accounting can be employed to give a favourable earnings picture. An example are companies that defer their earnings. They would report a reduced net income in one year, and save up the income to boost next year's earnings. So, if they don't perform as well the next year, it still gives the illusion of increasing earnings, thus predictable growth. There are a plethora of accounting shenanigans that can be used to increase earnings, giving the illusion that the company is doing better than it is.

Cash Flow Statement

'You can follow the action, which gets you good pictures. You can follow your instincts, which will probably get you in trouble. Or, you can follow the money, which nine times out of ten will get you closer to the truth.' Jack Nicholson

The way to circumvent creative accounting, is like Jack Nicholson says, by following the money. We can do this using the cash flow statements. Cash flow tells us what cash enters the business. It also tells us what cash is leaving the business, and how management are spending the company's cash.

	September 24, 2022
Cash, cash equivalents and restricted cash, beginning balances	$ 35, 929
Operating activities:	
Net income	99,803
Adjustments to reconcile net income to cash generated by operating activities:	
Depreciation and amortization	11,104
Share-based compensation expense	9,038
Deferred income tax expense/(benefit)	895
Other	111
Changes in operating assets and liabilities:	
Accounts receivable, net	(1,823)
Inventories	1,484
Vendor non-trade receivables	(7,520)
Other current and non-current assets	(6,499)
Accounts payable	9448
Deferred revenue	478
Other current and non-current liabilities	5,632
Cash generated by operating activities	122,151

Figure 6:10: Apple – Cash Flow Statement.

In Figure 6:10, below **Net income** which is the accounting figure, is **Adjustments to reconcile net income to cash generated**. These are all the adjustments made to reflect actually what cash entered Apple's pockets. There are certain things that Apple have to redact from their earnings, which hasn't happened in physical cash. This doesn't mean these things are irrelevant or unimportant. To give an example, **Depreciation and amortisation** refers to writing down assets based on their lifetime of usefulness. Let's imagine we are a printing company. In 2010, we spent £10 million on printers that will need changing in ten years. We can either take a huge hit on our earnings in 2010 (showing an income reduced by £10 million), so it appears we had a terrible year, which would happen every ten years we have to buy printers. Alternatively, we could 'amortise' it over its lifespan. So instead of reducing £10 million from our earnings in one year and nothing

84

from the next nine years of earnings, we split that £10 million over the ten years, taking £1 million from each year. This gives a better indication of the company's earnings over the ten-year period. Our balance sheet will have £10 million in the assets column in 2010 (when the printers were newly bought), which every year will be reduced by £1 million until it gets fully written off. The earnings will be reduced by £1 million each year too. The cash statement, however, will show the £10 million reduction in 2010, but nothing for the next nine years, as technically all the cash was paid in 2010 (assuming the printers were paid for in full). Another item is **Accounts payable**, which refer to accounts that need to be paid and have come off the earnings, but have not actually been paid yet. It is worth noting the discrepancies in earnings and cash influx, which is listed at the bottom as **Cash generated by operating activities**.

The second reason to look at a cash flow statement is to see how the management spend the company's cash.

Investing activities:	
Purchases of marketable securities	(76,923)
Proceeds from maturities of marketable securities	29,923
Proceeds from sales of marketable securities	37,446
Payments for acquisition of property, plant and equipment	(10,708)
Payments made in connection with business acquisitions, net	(306)
Other	(1,780)
Cash used in investing activities	(22,354)
Financing activities:	
Payments for taxes related to net share settlement of equity awards	(6,223)
Payments for dividends and dividend equivalents	(14,841)
Repurchases of common stock	(89,402)
Proceeds from issuance of term debt, net	5,465
Repayments of term debt	(9,543)
Proceeds from/(Repayments of) commercial paper, net	3,955
Other	(160)
Cash used in financing activities	(110,749)
Decrease in cash, cash equivalents and restricted cash	(10,952)
Cash, cash equivalents and restricted cash, ending balances	$ 24,977

Figure 6:11: Apple – Company Spending.

Apple have spent money on their **Investing activities**, mainly in **Purchases of marketable securities**, which we see as **marketable securities** on the balance sheet. They also bought property/equipment. In the financing activities, the most noteworthy items include **Payments for dividends**, and **Repurchases of common stock**. At the end we have the **Decrease in cash**, showing a reduction in cash holdings of $10.9 million. The last line is the amount of **Cash and cash equivalents** Apple has, which will also correlate with their figure in the current assets section of the balance sheets.

We now should understand that a company's figure for **earnings** is an accounting figure, whereas its **cash flow** is a true figure. We will examine a company called JCPenney (JCP) to illustrate the significance of analysing both when deciding to invest in a company. In 2019 JCP posted negative earnings. Using Figure 6:12 you will see a negative operating income of £8 million, which after debt payments becomes a net loss of $268 million.

(In millions, except per share data)	2019
Total net sales	$ 10,716
Credit income and other	451
Total revenues	11,167
Costs and expenses/(income):	
Cost of goods sold (exclusive of depreciation and amortization shown separately below)	7,013
Selling, general and administrative (SG&A)	3,585
Depreciation and amortization	544
Real estate and other, net	(15)
Restructuring and management transition	48
Total costs and expenses	(11,175)
Operating income/(loss)	(8)
Other components of net periodic pension and postretirement benefit cost/(income)	(35)
(Gain)/loss on extinguishment of debt	(1)
Net interest expense	293
Income/(loss) before income taxes	(265)
Income tax expense/(benefit)	3
Net income/(loss)	$ (268)

Figure 6:12: JCPenney – Sales and Expenses.

Its cash flow on the other hand paints a different picture. Figure 6:13 shows a positive cash flow from operating activities of $428 million. This is a stark difference from the loss of $268 million as earnings. The difference is mostly due to depreciation and amortisation, and usage of inventory, which as discussed above isn't a true cash cost, so is not deducted from the cash statement. It does represent cash invested in the past, however, so is not irrelevant.

($ in millions)	2019
Cash flows from operating activities	
Net income/(loss)	$ (268)
Adjustments to reconcile net income/(loss) to net cash provided by/(used in) operating activities:	
Restructuring and management transition	23
Asset impairments and other charges	
Net gain on sale of non-operating assets	(1)
Net gain on sale of operating assets	(8)
(Gain)/loss on extinguishment of debt	(1)
Depreciation and amortization	544
Benefit plans	(37)
Stock-based compensation	11
Other comprehensive income tax benefits	
Deferred taxes	(6)
Change in cash from:	
Inventory	271
Prepaid expenses and other assets	(9)
Merchandise accounts payable	(61)
Income taxes	
Accrued expenses and other	(30)
Net cash provided by/(used in) operating activities	428

Figure 6:13: JCPenney Cash Flows

The following parts of the cash statement in Figure 6:14 show cash lost from investing and debt financing activities, bringing a final increase in cash holdings of $53 million. Bear in mind this is not me saying that this company was a good buy, because it was 'secretly' making cash (when the earnings tell us the opposite). It's me getting across that earnings and cash flow need to be looked at judiciously, and not always taken at face value. In the case of JCPenney, the discrepancy in cash flow and earnings was due to standard accounting practices. They ended up declaring bankruptcy in 2020 due to negative cash flows and inability to service their high debts.[1] There are other cases where the opposite is true, and earnings are bolstered to paint a favourable picture. In these cases, scrutiny of both earnings and cash flow statements are advisable, to ascertain where the 'earnings' have come from.

Cash flows from investing activities	
Capital expenditures	(309)
Proceeds from sale of non-operating assets	1
Proceeds from sale of operating assets	26
Joint venture return of investment	
Insurance proceeds received for damage to property and equipment	6
Net cash provided by/(used in) investing activities	(276)
Cash flows from financing activities	
Proceeds from issuance of long-term debt	
Proceeds from borrowings under the credit facility	2,645
Proceeds of borrowings under the credit facility	(2,645)
Premium on early retirement of debt	
Payments of finance leases and note payable	(3)
Payments of long-term debt	(97)
Financing costs	
Proceeds from stock issued under stock plans	2
Tax withholding payments for vested restricted stock	(1)
Net cash provided by/(used in) financing activities	(99)
Net increase/(decrease) in cash and cash equivalents	53
Cash and cash equivalents at beginning of period	333
Cash and early equivalents at end of period	$ 386

Figure 6:14: JCPenney.

Income Ratios

The first two income ratios we will cover both have the same numerator, the share price. It's used as a measure of how much of a premium (or discount) one pays for a company's earnings. The most commonly used ratio is the price to earnings ratio.

---

1 The company had multiple years of negative cash flows, with 2019 being as exception. In 2018 and 2017, they had cash outlays of $125 and $429 million respectively.

Colloquially known as the P/E. As the name suggests, it's the price of a share, divided by the earnings attributed to that share:

$$\text{Price to Earnings} = \frac{Market\ price\ of\ the\ share}{Earnings\ per\ share}$$

NB – You can also use total market capitalisation (the price of all the shares of the company) divided by the total earnings. Using this, one would arrive at the same figure as above.

It's a measure of how many years it would take the share to make back its money in earnings. The higher the P/E, the more of a premium we pay for a company and vice versa. For example, when buying a property, you may look for the rent to pay off the price of the property in twenty years. This would give it a P/E of twenty. If the property gives a P/E of ten years, then either you bought it for a very good price (a lower P value), or the rent is unusually high (a higher E value). If we are interested in a company, we want to pay the lowest P/E we can for it. That just means we are getting it at the cheapest price. This does NOT mean that we should only invest in companies with low P/E ratios. We will expand on this below.

For equities (stocks), we went over the two ways you get financial benefit in Chapter 1, dividend or capital appreciation. The P/E that an investor pays for a stock, is normally based on the amount of growth a company is expected to undergo. This is because growth will give increased share prices, and hence greater capital appreciation.

Let's compare two companies in a similar industry. Ford Motor (F) and Tesla (TSLA). Ford Motor's history dates back to the creation of the first car by American inventor Henry Ford. It is one of the top five biggest car companies in the world, currently selling at a P/E of 4.5. On the other hand, Tesla's P/E is

140! The reason in the difference in valuation is the anticipated growth that investors seem to envisage with TSLA. Whereas for Ford, they see a much more stable company, with limited growth prospects. This is reflected by the lower price to earnings ratio. Now don't get me wrong, Tesla are the pioneers of electric cars, and their leader Elon Musk is a true visionary. However, how can we justify a P/E of 140 for what is at face value a car company? A car company which currently is getting a lot of competition when it comes to electric cars. In my opinion, Tesla is wildly overvalued, and at this P/E, I would not touch it. Tesla's share has beaten everyone's expectations, however. To quote Charlie Munger (Warren Buffett's business partner): "I would never buy Tesla, and I would never short it."

Let's look at another company that I have just bought. GlaxoSmithKline (GSK) is one of the largest pharmaceutical companies in the world. The larger the company, the harder it is to grow. We will go more into why in Part 4. GSK is a very stable company that spends a lot on R&D. They are constantly releasing new drugs into the market. On top of this they pay a dividend of 6.3%. The prospect of a healthy dividend and steady growth may be an attractive investment for people looking for a lower risk option than a company with a sky-high valuation like Tesla. GSK has a P/E of 9, which I would consider a good price. A simple way to look at what P/E one should pay is to compare it to the industry average. For automobiles, the average P/E is 5.25, which is higher than Ford but much lower than Tesla.

TASK – Look through GSK's 2022 Annual report. Have a look at the company's balance sheet, income statement and cash flows. Do you agree with my assessment of the company?

You will see many other metrics relating share price to another figure. One you may see is Price to Sales, or P/S. This can be useful, though it doesn't take into account the operating profit margin of a company. If the company has a low OPM, with large operating costs, then a large sales number becomes a significantly smaller earnings number. What appears as a low P/S, and a fair price for a company, can have a larger P/E than expected. As we mentioned earlier, tech stocks maintain a high profit margin due to the lower operating costs. The tech giant Microsoft, has a P/S of 9.5 and a P/E of 28. Compare this to the National Grid, which is a commodity company that supplies electricity to the UK and US. Their P/S is 1.7, though their P/E is 11.6. Microsoft has a P/E which is under three times more than its P/S. Whereas the National Grid, with its unsurprisingly large operating costs in infrastructure, has a P/E nearly seven times higher than its P/S.

A metric which I find more useful than P/S is Price to Free cash flow (P/FCF), as this looks at how much cash a company makes to fund activities that ultimately create value for the shareholders. To calculate this we take the total value of the shares (market capitalisation), aka the Price, and divide this by the Operating Free Cash Flow.

$$Price\ to\ Free\ Cash\ Flow = \frac{Market\ capitalisation}{Operating\ cash\ flow}$$

To calculate this for Apple we need to find the Operating Free Cash flow, which can be found in the cash flow statement. Take thirty seconds and see if you can find this number. It's the bottom number in Figure 6:10, under **Cash generated by operating activities**. This is the true cash influx into the business, if we don't take into account the other non-cash expenses like amortisation and depreciation etc.

$$Apple's\ Price\ to\ Free\ Cash\ Flow = \frac{\$3000,000,000,000}{122,151,000,000} = 24.6$$

Efficiency Ratios

These ratios tell us how efficiently a business is run. The best way to use these ratios is to compare the numbers to other businesses in the sector, and to its previous years. A business that has much higher ratios then its competitors, suggests it's a well-run and efficient business.

The operating profit margin, which we discussed above, tells us how well the business reduces costs to maximise their profits. Remember we can use gross or net income. Here's the equation again:

$$Gross/Net\ Operating\ Profit\ Margin\ (OPM) = \frac{Gross/Net\ income}{Net\ sales}$$

The other ratio we can look at is the company's returns relative to its assets. Like all ratios, it allows us to compare two companies of different sizes. A larger company may earn more than a smaller company as it has more assets on its balance sheet. However, it may deploy these assets much less efficiently than the smaller company.

To calculate this, we need to look at the income statement

$$Return\ on\ Assets = \frac{Net\ income}{Total\ assets} \times 100$$

To explain this let's go through a scenario. Company A earns £1,000 a year on assets of £10,000, and Company B earns £100 a year on assets of £700. Let's compare the ROAs for both companies:

$$ROA\ Company\ A\ =\ \frac{1000}{10,000} \times 100 = 10\%$$

$$ROA\ Company\ B\ =\ \frac{100}{700} \times 100 = 14\%$$

From analysing the results, it's clear that Company A is the more valuable company. It earns ten times the amount Company B does. However, Company B is the more efficient company based on its ROA.

One thing to look out for when calculating ROA are businesses that artificially inflate the value of their assets. This will give a lower ROA value than is true.

You may also see ROE, which stands for Return on Equity. Instead of using the assets as the denominator, it uses the shareholder equity. This is the assets minus the liabilities such as debt etc. I do not like using ROE as it doesn't take into account debt (as it is subtracted from assets to give equity). Companies take on debt to generate income, so I want it to be included in any calculation related to efficiency. Companies which are heavily indebted will have a much higher ROE compared to their ROA. Let's use the above examples again. Company A has taken on debts making up 50% of its assets, whereas Company B has no liabilities at all.

Company A
Total Assets = £10,000
Liabilities (debts) = £5,000 (50% of its assets)
Equity = £10,000 - £5,000 = £5,000

Company B
Total Assets = £700
Liabilities = £0
Equity = £700

$$ROE\ Company\ A\ = \frac{1,000}{5,000} \times 100 = 20\%$$

In the above scenario, the ROE for Company A has now doubled compared to its ROA. Company B on the other hand has an ROA equal to its ROE. You can see that on comparison of ROE, Company A would appear to be more efficient than Company B, as its debts are not taken into account. For this reason I don't use ROE, as it doesn't paint the full picture.

We have covered a lot in this chapter, so don't be surprised if it was a lot to digest. If some of it was confusing, don't worry! We are going to expand on some of the concepts discussed above in Part 4. In Chapter 17 we go through both qualitative and quantitative analysis of some case studies, which will nicely summarise all the things we covered in this chapter. If accounting is something that interests you, you may want to read through this chapter again; and if you haven't already, do some of the **Tasks** in this chapter. By taking the initiative and perusing through financial statements yourself, the learning will be cemented.

Below is an extra efficiency ratio which I have included for those who are more interested in accounting. If you aren't then please skip this and move to the next chapter (try completing the first two parts of the task at the bottom before you move on). We already discussed two of the important efficiency ratios which are OPM and ROA. Another efficiency ratio we can calculate is ROIC. This stands for Return on Invested Capital. ROIC tell us how efficiently a business allocates its capital to profitable investments. If you recall from Chapter 5, we discussed the importance of evaluating the ability of a company's management to effectively deploy capital in a way that increases profits. I'll go over the calculations below. It does get a bit complicated, so if it's a bit confusing then don't worry, as there are plenty of sources you can use to find out a company's ROIC.

$$Return\ on\ Capital\ Invested\ (ROIC) = \frac{Net\ Operating\ Profit\ after\ taxes\ (NOPAT)}{Invested\ Capital} \times 100$$

The calculation of ROIC is not as simple as ROA, as it does take into account the cost of capital.[1] This includes company debts which are interest bearing. To calculate this, we will breakdown how to calculate NOPAT and Invested capital separately.

$$NOPAT = Operating\ Income \times (1 - Tax\ rate)$$

For Company C

Net income = £30,000

Tax expense = £6,000

Operating Income[2] = £70,000

NB: All the above figures can be found on the income statement.

---

1 In Chapter 11 we will talk about discounted cash flow analysis which will make reference to cost of capital or WACC.

2 'Operating Income' is the earnings from the business operations minus the expenses directly related to business operation. It does not deduct interest or tax expenses which are taken to account in net income calculations.

$$Tax\ rate = \frac{Tax\ expense}{Net\ income} = \frac{£6,000}{£30,000} = 0.2\ \text{(which equates to a 20\% tax rate)}$$

$$NOPAT = £70,000\ x\ (1-0.2) = £56,000$$

Invested capital is calculated by the shareholder equity plus the interest-bearing debt. We then subtract the cash holdings of the business from this, as this is capital which has not been 'invested'.

All the figures below can be found from the balance sheet:

Current Liabilities:
Short term borrowings = £25,000

Non-Current Liabilities:
Long term borrowings = £750,000

Equity:
Shareholder Equity = £43,000

Cash Holdings:
Cash and cash equivalents = £15,000

Capital Invested = (£25,000 + £750,000 + £43,000) – £15,000
= £803,000

$$ROIC = \frac{NOPAT}{Invested\ Captial}\ x\ 100 = \frac{£56,000}{£803,000}\ x\ 100 = 6.97\%$$

TASK – Well done if you got the end of that! Now go through an Apple annual report and see if you can calculate the OPM, ROA and ROIC. You can use the Apple financial statements included above in this chapter.

PART 3

MACROECONOMICS

Macroeconomics is the study of the bigger picture. It's the study of the overall economy, the environment in which all companies exist. Things like inflation, interest rates, rate of economic growth, unemployment levels all come under the purview of macroeconomics. These are big topics that can have a drastic effect on share prices. The analysis of financial statements in the last chapter is what we call a bottom-up approach. Analysing the specifics of a company (microeconomics), its earnings, cash flow, operating margin etc. It doesn't look at the industry as a whole and takes the view that a company can still do well, even in an underperforming industry.

The angle we will take in this chapter is the top-down approach, thinking of the type of industry that a company is involved in, and how economic factors can influence this industry's performance. A good example is nightclubs during COVID. In the lockdowns of COVID, if you used a bottom-up approach and found a nightclub company with the greatest microeconomics, you would be naive not to consider the macroeconomic impact of a lockdown on nightclubs, which in the UK, was devastating. I use a top-down approach to help me find the type of industries that I want to be involved in. Then I use a bottom-up approach to find the companies within that industry which are the gems. If I don't know enough about the industry to carry out a bottom-up approach, I either don't invest, find an expert in the field, or use ETFs (see Chapter 3) to capture any general industry gains.

Macroeconomics is a humongous subject, but I'll address some of the key concepts that are often mentioned in financial outlets. At the time of writing, we are just coming out of peak COVID pandemic. With the significant effect COVID has had on the economy, macroeconomics is more important than ever.

Chapter 7
Interest Rates and Inflation

Interest rates refer to the percentage of the amount borrowed, which is paid by the borrower, for the lending of money. Put simply, if you borrow £100 from a bank, and they offer you an interest rate of 10%, you will pay back £110 (10% of £100 = £10. Then add £10 to the principal amount of £100 = £110). For those of you that have a variable mortgage on a house, you will know that interest rates fluctuate. They fluctuate depending on the monetary policy of the government. They alter interest rates to stimulate or stifle the economy. The way this works is as follows: the government lends money to the banks, who then go on to lend money to the public. So, if we are going to the bank for a loan, we have to bear in mind that they themselves are lending from the government (in the USA – Federal reserve, in the UK – Bank of England). If the government gives them a low interest rate on their borrowings, then they in turn are able to pass on that low rate to the customers. At the time of COVID, the Bank of England reduced rates to 0.1%, whereas now it stands at 4%. I'm sure you can appreciate that the rates for mortgages during the pandemic were much lower than they are now. Understandably, the banks will pass this increased rate of borrowing onto the customer.

What impact do interest rates have on the economy? During COVID lockdown, people weren't going out as much, they weren't spending as much, and many businesses were suffering. The economy was heading for a recession. To stimulate the economy the government lowered interest rates to 0.1%. This means that it cost much less to borrow. As borrowing gets cheaper for the banks, they can make borrowing cheaper for public consumers. Consumers are incentivised to spend and thus pump money into the economy, as the 'cost of money' is lower. To go back to the £100 analogy above, at 0.1% it would only cost 10 pence to borrow £100. With the £10 we paid earlier, we could get £10,000 in a low interest rate environment.

Lower interest rates don't just increase what consumers spend in the shopping malls. It extends to housing, travelling and even investments. When the cost of borrowing is less, it helps businesses and start-ups grow. Start-ups need capital to get going. If the cost of capital is less, they have a much higher chance of survival. The stock market also benefits, as consumers invest in the stocks, and make riskier plays due to the lower cost of borrowing. If you were to borrow money at 4%, and you invest it in the stock market you would have to make sure you generated more than that 4%, so you may be more risk-averse than if the borrowed money was only 0.1%. Hence why companies that don't have established earnings (like start-ups) benefit, as they are riskier investments. Riskier investments benefit from what we call an easy monetary policy (low cost of borrowing).

I'm sure some of you are wondering why the government doesn't keep interest rates low. After all, economic growth is the goal of all countries. As with all things in life, nothing is free. If rates are kept too low for too long, we have to deal with inflation…

Inflation

Currently in 2022/2023, inflation is a hot topic. It's the taboo word that is bad news for most people. Inflation is the decline in value of a currency over time. Purchasing power, which is what one can buy with their money, decreases. To give you some context, in 1860, what you could buy for £1, you would need £155 in today's money. So that carton of milk you buy for £1.50, would have cost less than 1 pence back in 1860. What can you buy for 1 penny nowadays? Let's talk about how inflation happens, and how it relates to interest rates.

To explain why inflation happens, we need to understand the relationship between price and supply-demand. As a producer, you would try to match your supply with your demand. If you were to open a trendy pastry shop, and you are selling out by midday, then you may want to increase the supply (in this case number of pastries) to meet the popular customer demand. Vice versa, if you have lots of pastries left over that you have to bin, it means your supply is exceeding your demand.

To explain how this analogy relates to price of the item, let's use limited edition trainers. All the kids in school seem to be obsessed with buying and reselling trainers. The way this works is all to do with the supply-demand ratio. Manufacturers intentionally make the supply of trainers fall far short of the demand for trainers. This keeps the prices high, as the demand is higher than the supply. Let's say you want to buy trainers, and you can only get them from one buyer, they can charge a high price as they are in limited supply. If there were loads of the shoes out there for sale, you could shop around, causing the suppliers to undercut one another thus reducing the price. If you try to charge the same high prices as before, people will just go to another supplier.

It is the same with money. If the supply of money exceeds

demand, it becomes worth less. In this example, demand is the rate of economic growth. The question I'm sure you are wondering is how the supply of money is increased. It's not like telling the factory to make more Yeezys (ask your kids if you don't know what these are). The government can print more money, which you will know if you have watched *Money Heist* on Netflix. The reason they do this is to pump money into the economy, to support the growing population, to pay off its debts on money it has borrowed, and to pay for cost of crisis such as a world war or a pandemic. By increasing the supply excessively, as was the case during COVID, you increase the supply more than the demand. By doing this, money becomes worth less. The important thing to note is that for inflation to occur, the money printed has to be 'lent and spent.' If the money doesn't make its way to the economy, then technically you won't get inflation. If you don't understand this, let me present it as a real-life scenario. The government prints money and lends it to the banks. The banks now lend all this printed cash to people willing to buy a house. Now multiple people can afford to buy this house. Because there are lots of customers willing to buy the house (aka increased demand), then the person selling the house can start to charge more for the house (as the supply for houses isn't going to suddenly increase, as printing money takes much less time than building houses). In this way housing prices will go up in value. Alternatively, you could say that the money becomes worth less, as it takes more money to get the same thing. It is the same story with supermarkets selling milk. As the farmers' rent, electricity etc go up, their cost to produce the milk goes up. So, they charge the supermarket more, the supermarket increases the price they sell it to us, and the person that owns a coffee shop increases their prices as the milk now costs more. You can see in this example how increasing the price at the top sets off an almost chain reaction, which results in everyone suddenly increasing their prices for the exact same service. This is inflation simplified.

To relate this to interest rates, if the interest rate is decreased, then everyone wants to borrow. This means more money is lent and spent, which means supply increases and money loses its purchasing power. If governments keep interest rates suppressed for too long, inflation can run wild. Hence why after all the stimulus cheques and money printing that occurred during COVID, governments are raising interest rates. They do this to reduce the supply of money entering the economy, thus reducing the rate of inflation. The downside is that it acts as a dampener on economic growth. You could say the government are stuck between a rock and a hard place when it comes to the toss-up between curbing inflation and supporting the economy.

In times of inflation, the money we have sitting in our bank account is becoming less valuable by the rate of inflation. When we look for yields achievable in investing (how much we make from investing an amount), we want it to be greater than the rate of inflation. For example, if inflation is 8%, and the government bonds we talked about in Chapter 2 is 1.5%, then what we call our 'real' yield, or inflation adjusted yield is -6.5% (1.5% - 8%= -6.5%). We would have a negative yield, so we would be 'losing' money. The reason I put losing in quotation marks is because our portfolio would still numerically grow by 1.5%, but the actual value of the money would decrease. In times of high inflation, investors may look for investments that generate higher returns, in order to beat inflation. In the US, there are bonds which are inflation protected. They are known as TIPS (Treasury Inflation Protected Securities). These will give the investor the 'real' rate of return, as the yield they pay out increases/decreases based on the fluctuation of inflation rates.

Investors may also look for inflation-proof businesses. One of which being commodities. With businesses selling a commodity such as oil, or corn, the supplier simply increases the prices to keep up with inflation. In this way farmers' business profits aren't affected by the increased costs of water etc. For a business with high competition, who can't increase their prices as easily, they will be hurt by inflation. This is because their cost to produce the product may increase, but the price at which they sell the product will not increase by the same amount.

Yield Curve

Above we discussed the effect that interest rates and inflation can have on an economy, and how varying macroeconomic conditions may alter our investment decisions. A useful clue to what the future economic conditions might look like can be found in the prices of bonds. The indicator we use is called the yield curve. This curve compares the price of shorter-term to longer-term bonds.

To explain the yield curve, we need to understand the relationship between interest rates, bond prices and bond yields. Firstly, the latter two. As bond prices decrease, their yields increase. This is because a bond pays out a fixed amount. No matter what price you buy it at, you still get paid the same amount. So, when bond prices fall, their yield increases and vice versa. Now, how do interest rates correlate bond prices and yields? As interest rates increase, bond prices decrease (so bond yields increase). This is because when the government raises interest rates, they issue new bonds that match the new higher interest rate. This makes all the old bonds less valuable as they have a lower yield compared to the new bonds. The old bonds thus fall in price, effectively increasing their yield in response to risk of higher interest rates.

As you will recall from Chapter 2, bonds have a range of different maturities (expiry dates), ranging from months to decades. In a normal environment, the yield of the longer-term bonds have a higher yield than the shorter-term bonds. This is only fair, as you have your money tied up for longer, so deserve to be rewarded with a higher yield. As you can see from Figure 7.1, the normal yield curve rises steadily until it plateaus at the higher maturities.

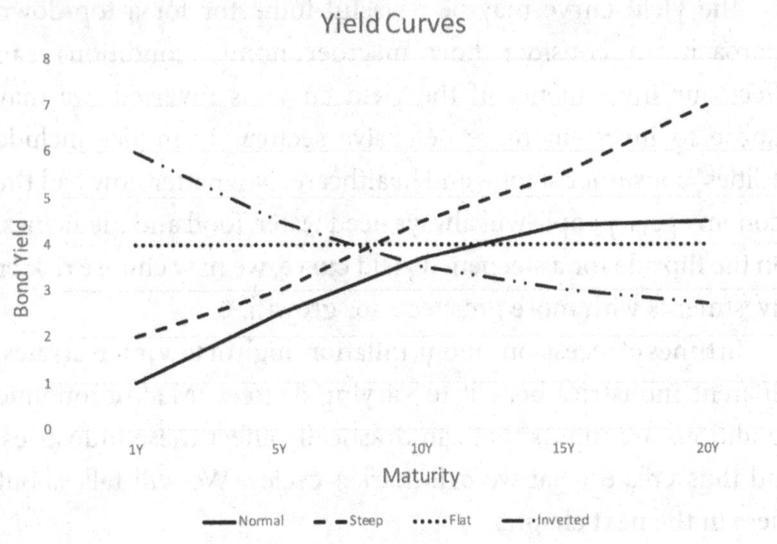

The next type of yield curve is the steep curve. This curve has higher bond yields when compared to the normal curve, and also doesn't plateau at the higher maturities. This indicates that we have favourable economic conditions, anticipating growth in the market. As we learnt from above, excessive growth may be accompanied by inflation, which leads to an increase in interest rates to keep inflation under control. As the interest rates are predicted to increase in the future, the longer-term bonds will decrease in price and hence increase in yield as we see from the steepened curve.

The flat curve can be seen in times of high uncertainty. When the bond market is unsure about what the future entails, the yields of all maturities are similar, as they are unable to predict whether we will see higher or lower interest rates in the future.

The inverse yield curve is the last type, which is very rare, though was last inverted this year in 2022. This type of curve means that shorter-term bonds give a higher yield than longer-term bonds. This is a sign of severe slowdown in the economy and is a very reliable indicator of an incoming recession.

The yield curve may be a useful indicator for a top-down approach, to consider how macroeconomic conditions can affect our investments. If the yield curve is inverted, we may choose to invest in more defensive sectors. Examples include utilities, consumer staples and healthcare. No matter how bad the economy gets, people will always need water, food and medicines. On the flipside for a steepened yield curve, we may choose riskier investments with more prospects for growth.

In times of recession, boom, inflation, high or low interest rates, different industries benefit to varying degrees. Macroeconomic conditions are inputs that can drastically affect these industries, and thus create what we call market cycles. We will talk about these in the next chapter.

TASK – Identify what type of yield curve is currently present. To find the yield curve, just type in yield curve and your country.

Chapter 8
Market Cycles

Market cycles are trends that occur as a result of certain stimuli. These stimuli can cause stocks of a certain sector to outperform other stocks, or cause certain asset classes to outperform others. Each cycle can be split into four phases.

1. **Accumulation**

    This is the first stage of the market cycle when the early investors begin to accumulate stock. Typically, in this stage, fewer retail investors are buying this share due to the 'lack of action' in the share price.[1]

2. **Markup**

    This is when the buyers start to dominate the sellers. The market is now in an uptrend, forming 'higher highs' and 'higher lows.' This upward movement can attract attention, leading to a greater volume of buyers, which creates further increases in share price.

---

1 'Retail investor' is a term used to describe the individual investors who buy securities for their own personal accounts (like me and you!). This is in contrast to the Institutional investors, who are the 'big fish'. These are the pension fund and hedge fund managers that manage large amounts of money for their clients.

3. **Distribution**

    This stage signifies the peak of the cycle. It signals the reversal where the early buyers begin converting to sellers. At this point the volume of stock trading hands is usually the highest. However, the price does not increase, as late buyers are absorbing the sellers.

4. **Markdown**

    This is the point when the sellers start to dominate the buyers. The downtrend begins with 'lower highs' and 'lower lows.' This can lead to panic selling, causing a rapid drop in market price.

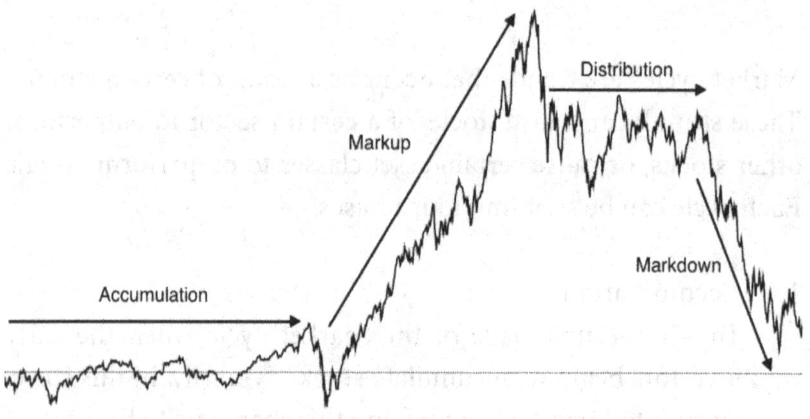

Figure 8:1: Stages of a market cycle.

Above is a chart showing the four stages of a market cycle in action. There is so much that can be said about market cycles and bubbles, but I will only give a brief overview of the topic. If you are interested in market cycles, I really recommend *Mastering the Market Cycle* by Howard Marks.

Credit Cycle

The credit cycle is one of the most important market cycles. Our economy runs on credit and taking on debt. The access to credit is what allows our economy to thrive. In times of low interest rates, companies can borrow cheaply, take on debts and expand their business. Importantly they are also able to refinance their debts. By this I mean any debts that are outstanding can be extended and renegotiated (preferably at a lower interest rate).

During the expansionary period of the credit cycle, interest rates are low, lending rules are laxer and more credit is available. This stimulates the economy, as more money pours into a greater number of hands. The number of investments in real estate and businesses increases. This drives up the prices of these assets, making more people willing to invest. As people's willingness to invest goes up, and banks are giving out credit freely, people invest with a higher risk tolerance. They make riskier investments as a result, buying securities of a lesser quality. Inevitably this continues until asset prices peak, and the mark-up phase ends.

At this point we may see start to see drops in asset prices from their peak. This may result in bankruptcy of overleveraged companies, as they are unable to survive the drop in asset prices. Banks then start to contract credit, tightening their lending requirements. Interest rates may rise causing the cost of debt to increase. This lack of credit availability means it becomes harder for companies to refinance their debts. This acts as a dampener on the economy, as there no longer access to the 'easy credit' with which the economy can grow. As a result, investors start to behave in a more risk-averse manner and less money flows into the market. As the number of sellers increases, there is a drop in asset prices. This drop in asset prices precipitates more selling and further reduction in prices. This is the last stage, or the markdown phase of the cycle discussed above. The cycle begins again when the government lowers interest rates, increasing the money supply and creating a flow of money into the market as discussed above.

Commodity Cycle

Let's look at another cycle, the commodity cycle. Commodities include all the raw materials of the world, such as the products of agriculture or mining. Examples include foodstuffs like grain, corn, and coffee, metals such as iron, copper or gold, and materials used to generate energy, such as crude oil and natural gas. Commodities can be traded on the open market, and they represent value which exists outside of the 'fiat' value. Fiat value refers to the value of money, which as we established above, can vary based on the rate of inflation and interest rates. Commodities have an intrinsic value due to their practical use. People need corn to eat, metal to build, and oil to meet energy demands. For these reasons they can have a degree of inflation proofness from fiat currency inflation and a weakening currency. To give an example, let's say you owned 1kg of grain worth £2. In an environment with high inflation of 10%, the £2 is no longer worth as much, as the currency is devalued by 10% per annum. Your 1kg of grain on the other hand, will still feed the exact same number of people, irrespective of the amount of currency inflation there was. With 10% inflation, this 1kg of grain is now worth £2.20. The currency gets 10% weaker and has 10% less buying power. Using this basic example, it is easy to see how buying commodities may be a good way to hedge (prepare yourself against) inflation. Rising inflation means rising commodity prices. Bear in mind that commodity prices are not invulnerable to inflation. There is a famous story of Mansa Musa (this is a true story – look him up), who was the king of Mali. He was one of the richest men in the world. On his way to the pilgrimage of Haj, he passed by Egypt and flooded the city with gold, giving it out to everybody. This rapid increase in supply caused the inflation of gold, meaning the price of gold in Egypt dropped for the following twelve years.

If one did want to invest in the commodity market, there are four principal ways to do so:

1. **Physical ownership**

   Physically owing the commodity. People commonly do this with precious metals such as gold or silver. They can buy gold or silver coins, bars, or as commonly practised within the Asian community, jewellery.

2. **Futures contracts**

   These work in a similar way to options (see Chapter 4), which involves betting on the future price of the raw material. When comparing futures and option contracts, the differences lie with the expiry date. When an option contract expires, it becomes immaterial. The contract is only acted upon if the option contract is actioned before expiry. The futures contract on expiry does not become void, it becomes actioned. If this is a bit confusing, then the take-home message is that futures contracts are simply betting on the future price of a commodity.

3. **Securities/shares**

   This provides indirect access to the commodities' price. If it's sugar that you want to invest in, you can purchase the stock of the company that grows the sugar cane, the one that processes it, or the one that sells it for consumption. If the price of sugar increases, then so do these companies' profits, and hence the share price.

4. **ETFs**

   We discussed ETFs in Chapter 3. There are many ETFs that

provide diversified exposure to a commodity of choice.

Commodities also move in cycles. We call this a commodity supercycle. The reason it is a supercycle is that unlike stocks and bonds, commodities typically move together in unison. They move in boom-and-bust cycles that extend over a long period of time, on average ten to fifteen years. What initiates these cycles is demand versus supply imbalances.

Unexpected demand shocks are the most common trigger of a commodity supercycle. A 1% increase in economic growth results in a 9.9% increase in commodity usage. The first commodity supercycle coincided with the industrialisation of America, and the second with the beginning of World War II. Both of these events caused sudden increases in demand, or a positive demand shock, resulting in a demand versus supply imbalance. As demand outweighs supply, the prices of commodities increase. In the event of a global recession or slowdown, we see reduced demand for commodities, or negative demand shocks. This results in a reduction in commodity prices, as was evident in the Great Recession of 2009 and the lockdowns in 2020.

Supply shocks, which are sudden changes in the supply of a commodity, can also precipitate a commodity market turning point. A good example is crude oil, which is commonly subject to negative supply shocks. Most of our crude oil comes from the Middle East. As this is a volatile region, disruptions in oil exportation cause a reduction of supply, and hence an increase in the price of commodities. Look at a recent event, Russia's invasion of Ukraine. This caused an increase in gas prices due to a reduction of supply relative to demand.

The commodity cycle lasts longer than other cycles. This is due to the high costs of producing commodities, and the slow supply response. This refers to the time taken for supply to increase to match the increased demand. As this is slower, the cycle also moves slower and takes longer, hence why it is known as a supercycle.

Real Estate Cycle

Although real estate is outside the purview of this book, it should come as no surprise that real estate is also subject to cycles. There are many that believe that real estate will 'always go up,' or 'everyone needs somewhere to live' and so on. This mindset can cause the public to pay higher prices for their homes. At times when mortgage rates are low, and mortgage products with enticing features like low initial monthly payments make houses more affordable, the demand for housing increases. This causes an increase in home sales. The rise in asset prices creates more enthusiasm, resulting in even higher asset prices and higher-risk investments. Unlike marketable securities that can be created relatively quickly to meet increased demand, homes take time to build. The increased demand is not met instantly by an increased supply. This creates a demand-supply imbalance, which results in further increases in real estate prices. This imbalance and price increase incentivises investors and homebuilders to start new projects. However, houses take time. They need planning permission, architectural designs, building etc. The time in between the increase in demand houses and the completion of these new housing projects is ample time for market conditions to sour. Contraction of the availability of credit or worsening of general economic conditions can cause demand for housing to drop. It can also lead to defaults and foreclosures, which will increase the supply of houses on the market. Projects that begin in good times when demand outweighs supply may find themselves being completed in bad times where supply now outweighs demand. This oversupply of houses results in property vacancies.

This puts a downward pressure on housing prices, resulting in a real estate market decline. In a real estate cycle, there are a couple of factors that can amplify the size of the bubble. Firstly, that financial leverage in real estate is the norm. Use of leverage means more money is invested, and the holder is more susceptible to drops in asset prices. Secondly, that supply cannot be adjusted as easily to meet demand, creating a greater imbalance when conditions change.

Market Bubbles

Bubbles are the result of a significant mark-up phase. When we think of market bubbles, we think of huge overvaluation followed by a crash and widespread ruin. In reality bubbles can be of any size. They don't have to affect the whole market, they can be limited to a niche asset class. An example of this is the Great British Bicycle Bubble of 1896. The invention of bicycles caused a bubble in bicycle stocks, which popped when low-cost American bicycles flooded the market, curtailing enthusiasm for bicycle stocks and precipitating a crash. If you want to read more about bubbles, then I highly recommend *Boom and Bust* by William Quinn and John D. Turner.

Let's take a look at an iconic bubble, the dot-com boom. This was the bubble of the year 2000. It was one of the most notorious bubbles, which, when it popped, caused a widespread bankruptcy and an economic recession. What caused the bubble was the psychological drive. This drive was caused by excitement about the internet, or what was then called the World Wide Web, that became available to the public. This represented a shift towards the digital world. The technology sector was the highlight of this narrative shift, so tech stocks were hot, and investors poured money into high-risk assets expecting growth. As the price of

118

shares increased, more investors put money in, dismissing the gross overvaluations. In hindsight we can easily say this was a terrible decision; however, when investors are seeing their colleagues' assets tripling, their clients leaving their funds as they aren't delivering the returns other care-free investors are, it becomes understandable why many succumbed to investing in overpriced assets. What allowed the bubble to be sustained was a government which created a favourable environment. Interest rates were low, which, as we learnt above, meant more money floating around the economy, and more to invest. Secondly, an act was passed in congress called the Taxpayer Relief Act of 1997. This lowered capital gains tax rates in the US, encouraging people to make investments that promised growth, hence more speculative investments. This loose monetary policy was the 'fuel' for the 'mark-up phase'. However, as the stocks became wildly overvalued, and there were no more buyers, sellers started to dominate the market. Investor psychology then starts to shift. No longer do people believe that the 'only way for the share is up.' This causes the share price to start dropping. The share price drop created more risk-averse investment mentality, resulting in more sell-offs. Because many of the investment funds were overleveraged, the drop in asset prices led to margin calls and more selling-off of assets. Investment funds and even banks which were too overleveraged were forced to declare bankruptcy. This led to a chain of bankruptcies and the ensuing recession. If you want to read more about the dot-com bubble in particular, then I recommend Dot.con by John Cassidy.

For bubbles to form, the two crucial components are the psychological drive, and the fuel to sustain the drive. The psychological component takes the form of investor excitement. Excitement about stocks that promise high returns allows investors to get carried away. Imbued with confidence in what is often a novel concept results in less risk-averse investing, at prices that are overvalued. These overvaluations are of no matter, as the psychology is that 'it will keep going up.' This mindset also leads to utilisation of leverage so as not to miss out on the investment 'opportunity of a lifetime.' The fuel that feeds this overleveraging is, as mentioned above, loose monetary policy which increases the availability of credit. The intensity of a bubble depends on the amount of drive and fuel available. In life what goes up must come down, hence the intensity of the ensuing crash depends on the size of the bubble. Governments will often act to pop a bubble before it gets too big and causes too catastrophic a crash. The way they do this is by raising interest rates, which is effectively cutting off the supply of fuel. As the cost of money increases, investors' psyche gets brought back down to earth, popping the bubble. The mindset then shifts to a negative outlook on stocks. The belief that 'there's no money to be made in the market' sends stock prices to all-time lows. When the prices are low enough, and the companies are selling at bargain prices, investors start buying in again, and the cycle starts again. Bubbles are truly inevitable, it is a part of human nature, and they will come and go many times in our lifetime.

Summary

Macroeconomics is a humongous topic, of which we have but scratched the surface. The take-home message is that top-down analysis, which is looking at the economic environment a business is in, may provide reason, or not, to invest in a stock. Economic conditions which may cause one asset class to thrive may at the same time cause another to underperform. An appreciation for these conditions would be prudent for any investor.

An understanding of market cycles can give the investor a bearing of where they might be in a cycle, and a direction of how conditions may change. Based on these predictions, a portfolio can be constructed to combat such eventualities. A proverb by Howard Marks summarises it best: "What a wise man does in the beginning, the fool does in the end." If we look at the dot-com bubble, investors that first invested in tech stocks are innovators, the ones that follow are the imitators, and the ones that come last are the idiots. In Chapter 11 we talk about value investing and being a contrarian. It's a way to ensure that you pay the correct price for a stock, and you are one of the innovators, not the fool investing at the end.

Here's an example of how I used macroeconomics to make an investment decision recently during COVID. The amount of money the government printed was overwhelming. Forty per cent of all US dollars in circulation were printed in the last year! For me, this rapid increase in money supply screamed inflation. This, alongside supply chain issues, is why I decided to invest in something that keeps its value. Something that would serve as a hedge against inflation. The commodities I chose were precious metals, gold and silver. The government has started tightening the supply by raising interest rates. This contraction of credit will reduce inflation, but will also bring about an economic recession. I believe the government will pause interest rate hikes and even consider reducing rates in order to stimulate the economy. By doing this they will accept a higher than ideal inflation rate, but prevent a full-blown recession. By the time you read this, you will know if I was correct in my assessment or not!

PART 4

INVESTING STRATAGEM

Chapter 9
Risk Management

Before we get onto the more exciting topics, we have to cover one of the most important tenants of investing, risk management. It is so fundamental for two reasons. Firstly, it allows an individual to safeguard their assets. It does this by limiting your downside. Secondly, it allows you to stay calm, rational, and keep your emotions out of your decision-making process. This may seem obvious to the mathematicians out there but consider this: if your portfolio suffers a 50% loss, it then takes a 200% gain just to get back to even! So, if your portfolio of £10,000 dropped by 50%, it is now valued at £5,000. To get back to your initial £10,000 investment you have to double your current portfolio of £5,000. This can take years to accomplish! If you're the ninety-year-old man from our introduction, those are years that you may physically not have. Hence Warren Buffett's two rules to investing: "The first rule of an investment is don't lose [money]. And the second rule of an investment is **don't forget the first rule**."

Now, you are probably thinking that if your stock went down by 50%, then you would just hold the stock until it goes back up to its initial price. Theoretically this is correct, as no monetary loss or gain is realised until the entity is sold.[1] However, what happens when you open your account and your portfolio is down by 60%, or 70%? At what point do you 'cry uncle' and decide to sell? Or as we say in the investing world, where's your 'uncle point'? Let me give you an example.

Figure 9:1: Three-year price-of-stock chart for Royal Mail 2018-2020.

Figure 9:1 is a three-year chart of the company Royal Mail from 2018 to 2020. If you are from the UK, this company needs no introduction. For those of you that aren't, it's the biggest parcel delivery company in the UK, shipping over a billion packages a year. The chart shows the price of one stock of the specified company. For now, ignore the other things on the chart. Its all-

---

1 This also raises an important point about tax. If your portfolio makes you a millionaire overnight, you don't pay a dime to the taxman unless you sell your shares. There are ways around this which we will delve into in Chapter 16.

time peak was around £630 per share, marked by the top purple line. Let's say you bought the share at £600 in 2018. It pays a decent dividend, and the company isn't going away anytime soon. So, you buy the share and the share price starts dropping. Because of the company's reputation you decide to hold the share. Now in hindsight, we can see that the share drops to around £125 around April 2020 (the bottom purple line). This is an 80% drop in your investment (which if you sold, would need a 500% gain to get back to parity). At what point in that journey do you hit your uncle point…? At what point do you decide you've made the wrong call and decide to cut the losses?

Let's say you're patient and choose to hold. Look at Figure 9:2, which covers the two years after 2020. You were right, the investment starts to go up again. It gets up to £591 around June 2021 and you decide to just wait a bit more till it gets to £600. After all, it has gone from £125 all the way to £591, so it's performing phenomenally. Lockdowns and COVID are easing, what could go wrong? After the peak at £591 you can see below it starts to decline. It is reasonable to think that this is normal since bull markets (markets that experience upward price movements) follow cyclical patterns. So, after an upward run they retrace (reduce in price), then continue on the run, then retrace again then continue and so on and so forth. So, you end up holding. Then a year goes by and it never hits £600, and is now valued at around £300. Do you sell or do you continue to hold? While there is no direct cost for holding a stock (despite minimal brokers' fees for holding a share on your behalf), consider the cost of lost opportunity. You have spent five years on a share which has decreased by 50%. If you chose not to sell, then how much longer are you going to tie up money that could be making so much more for you! This stock could spend the rest of your life never reaching the £600 level. My question to you is this, when do you sell? I want you to imagine yourself on the journey above and ask yourself, what would you have done from 2018 if you owned the stock but didn't have foresight? My answer to that is I have no idea, because I don't have a proper risk management strategy in place. Without a structured plan, I, like yourselves in this scenario, am running on emotions. This is the behaviour of a speculator.

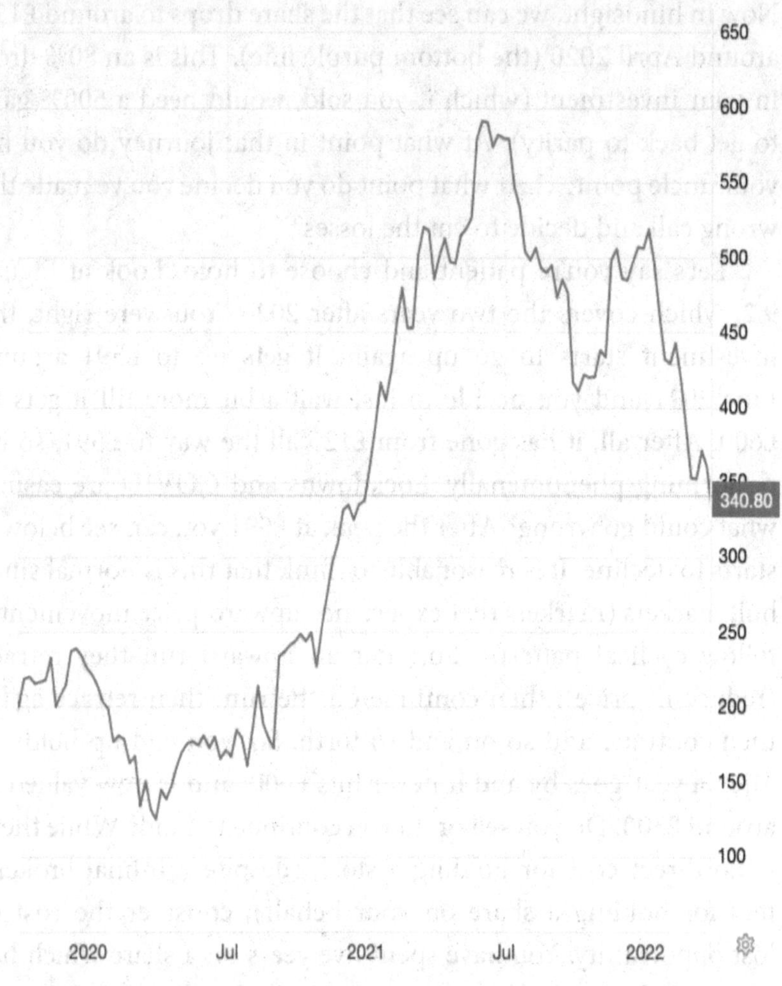

Figure 9:2: Three-year price-of-stock chart for Royal Mail 2020-2022

Now a few of you will be thinking why in the theoretical scenario are we buying Royal Mail at its peak, which is great, as

128

you're now starting to think like an investor! However, don't get too held up on the actual stock, as this was an exercise to show the importance of risk management, on both limiting downsides and structuring our decision-making process.

Stop Losses

Stop losses are like circuit breakers you can put into your trade. Its job is to get you out of the trade when it drops below a certain price level. When the stock hits the set price level, it will sell the investment, capping the loss at whatever amount was set. Let's say you buy a company whose shares are selling for £100, and you only want to lose a maximum of 10% on your investment. You will enter your stop loss in at £90, as this equates to a loss of 10% (10% of £100 pounds being £10. Take this away from £100 and you're left with £90 being your stop loss). If the stock reduces in value and reaches £90, then your investment will be sold, and your 10% loss will become 'realised'. If you only want to lose a maximum of £1,000 on your investment, then you would only buy 100 shares of the company at this stop loss price (as £10 loss per share, for 100 shares, would equal £1,000). If your stop loss was 20%, but you still only wanted to lose £1,000, then you would only buy fifty shares, as you are taking double the risk by changing your stop loss to a 20% loss (20% of £100 being £20 per share, 50 shares x £20 = £1,000).

At what level you put your stop loss depends on your reason for buying, your level of certainty and the level of risk that you wish to take with the investment in question. So, for investing in a stock which you wish to hand over to your grandchildren, you may not want to put a stop loss, as you never want to sell it. For a safe stock like the National Grid, you may want to put your stop loss at 30% of the price. For a riskier stock you may want to put an even tighter stop loss. Be wary though, as stocks can fluctuate massively. If you are very cautious and put too tight a stop loss, then you will keep getting 'stopped out'(when the price hits the amount set by the stop loss and your investment is sold) of your trades, taking small losses and potentially missing the ensuing bullish rally (upward movement). Take this example: had you bought a share of Amazon as a gift for your relative at the beginning of the year 2000, and put a 50% stop loss, they would have been stopped out, and realised a 50% loss on your initial investment. If, however, you had not put a stop loss, your relative would have instead made fifty times their money in the next twenty-one years. This is a rare example; however, the take-home point is to be selective with where you put your stop loss. I know what you're thinking, what maniac buys shares as a birthday present? That's what Warren Buffett buys his family as gifts!

For deciding what level to put your stop loss, you will gain more clarity in the upcoming chapters, as we delve deeper into investing stratagem. As a quick overview, consider why you're buying the stock, is it to keep forever? How much do you want to lose on the stock, how much of your money are you willing to risk? And lastly how volatile is the stock? If you want to buy bitcoin and you only want to lose 10% on the investment, then get ready to get stopped out very quickly. The chart in Figure 9:3 is the two-year chart for bitcoin – the price is all over the shop, with high volatility, which means high risk. To even enter this trade, you need a wide stop loss. Instinctively you will want a tighter stop loss, as the trade carries more risk. It presents us with a catch-22 in this case. Personally, I don't have a stop loss with my bitcoin holding, as my investing thesis is a hold-and-forget-about-it. We will cover cryptocurrency later in the book.

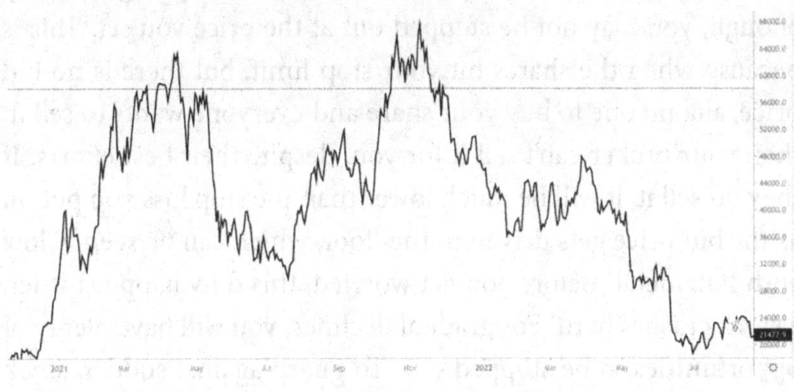

Figure 9:3: Two-year chart for Bitcoin – price of stock.

Let me give you an example of an investment I made in which a stop loss was crucial. I invested in Polymetal International, a Russian mining company, not long before the start of the chart below as Figure 9:4. I bought into the company around £13.15 and had held it for a year. Because it was situated in Russia, the investment carried what we call a geopolitical risk (a fancy word for risk that is attributable to the situation/stability of a country). For this reason, I put a stop loss at 20% – which was what I was willing to lose on this investment. While I did say above that riskier assets may need wider stop losses, the chart of Polymetal had no way near the volatility of bitcoin, so I was ok with a tighter stop on a trade which had inherent risk. Lo and behold Russia, or should I say Putin, decides to invade Ukraine. Luckily for me, my trade gets stopped out at around £10.50, just weeks before the huge crash. That was a 90% crash which I only avoided by placing a stop loss! I was then in a position to invest the money I freed up into Polymetal when it was at its low of £1.40, allowing me to sell it a few months later for an 80% gain.

Even if you have a stop loss, if the share drops significantly enough, you may not be stopped out at the price you set. This is because when the shares hit your stop limit, but there is no bid price, aka no one to buy your share and everyone wants to sell it, then your broker can't sell it for you, despite their best efforts. If they do sell it, it will be much lower than the stop loss you put in, as the bid price gets driven to the floor, which can be seen below with Polymetal. Before you get worried, this only happens when a stock crashes hard. For gradual declines, you will have plenty of opportunities to be stopped out. To guard against sudden stock crashes, some brokers offer something called guaranteed stop losses. This means that no matter what, you will be paid back as if the share was sold at the stop level you set. As we know, you won't actually be stopped out, the broker will just pay you as if you were. The brokerage will then shoulder the difference between what they paid you for the share and what they actually sold the share for. Obviously, a guaranteed stop costs more. It's a bit like adding anytime cancellation insurance to your travel tickets.

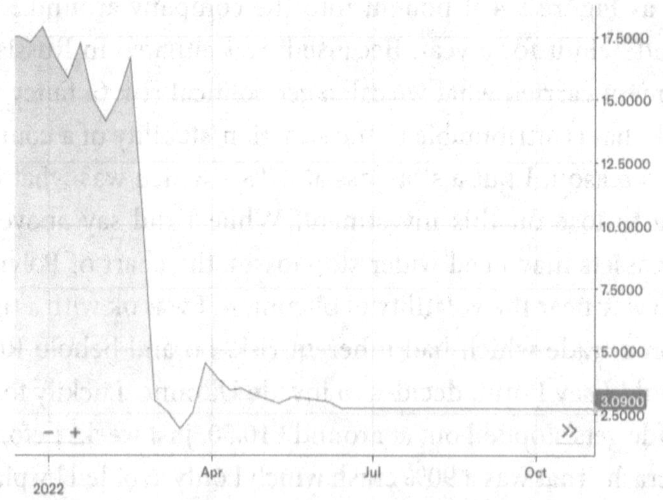

Figure 9:4: Polymetal – price of stock Jan to June 2022.

Stop losses are great as they protect your downside. However, what automated tools can we implement to help us capture the upside gains as well as protect our downside? I present to you 'trailing stops.' These are stops that go up as the stock price goes up, but then do not fall when the market does. Let me give you an example. You buy a share at £500. You set a trailing stop at 20%. This means you will be stopped out at a market price of £400. If your share price moves down to £420 or £460, then the stop loss stays where it is. If the price moves **above** £500 (your buy price), let's say to £520, then the trailing stop will move up to 20% of the new higher price (20% of £520 = £416). Even if the price moves down to below £500 again, the stop loss doesn't move, it will stay at the higher stop loss price of £416. It will only move if the price goes above the previous high of £520, or of course if it hits the new stop price of £416, in which case, the shares will be sold. This is an excellent way of capturing upside gains while protecting the downside.

Let's look at a stock for which I didn't put a stop loss, where a trailing stop might have been appropriate. Back in the height of COVID I invested in the Chinese large cap ETF.[1] The reason I bought this ETF was to invest in corporate China as a whole, as we discussed in Chapter 3. I bought it at the start of the Figure 9:5 chart in 2020, where it went on to make a gain of around 25%. China then decided to crack down on tech companies, incited by a remark from the owner of Alibaba (China's equivalent of Amazon), that criticised Chinese regulators for 'stifling innovation.' China is a communist country under authoritarian rule. This means that political opposition is suppressed, and civil

---

1 Large-caps refers to companies with a 'large capitalisation'. These are companies with market capitalisations of $10 billion or above. Mid-caps are companies between $2 - $10 billion, and Small-caps are between $250 million and $2 billion. Often institutional investors have limits on what they can purchase. A pension fund manager for example, may only be able to purchase Large-caps, as they are on the whole, a safer asset class then Small-caps.

rights are curtailed. Essentially, the government can do whatever the hell it wants, which is what it did. This reminded people of the geopolitical risk of doing business in China, which led to the ensuing decline seen from 2021. I overlooked the obvious risk inherent in China's political system and did not put any stop loss. A trailing stop would have worked well here. I would have locked in the gains from the bull run from 2020 to 2021, then been stopped out before suffering the big bearish move (bear represents markets decreasing in price). It would have allowed me to capture any gains, as well as giving me the option to buy in again at a lower and more attractive price.

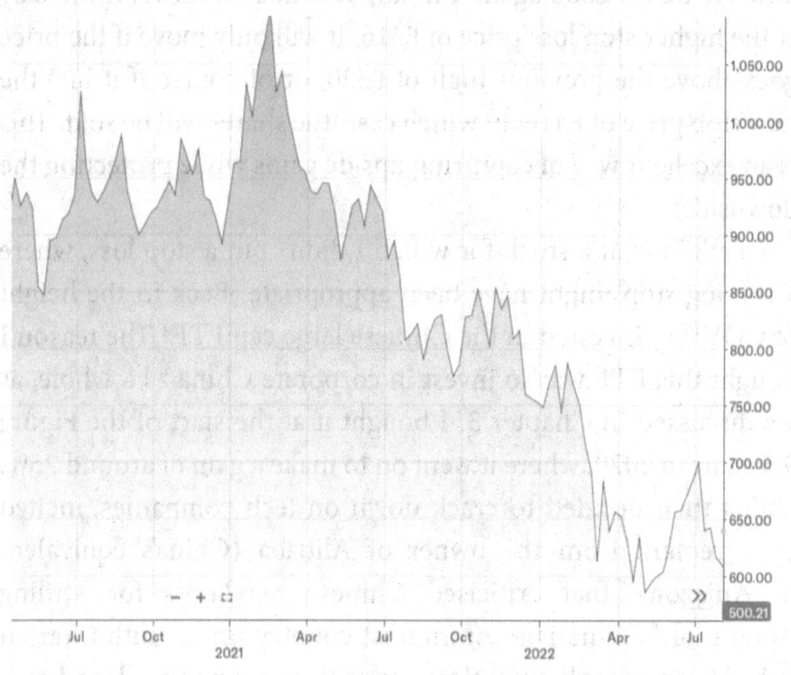

Figure 9:5: Share price of China large cap ETF from 2020 to 2022.

Limit Orders

I won't say much about limit orders, but they are worth mentioning as you will undoubtedly come across them. These are again automated ways to enter and exit the market. Let's say you want to buy a share of our esteemed Royal Mail. But you decide £600 is too high (good call!). You think £400 is more reasonable, but you don't want to check the market every day to see if it hits the level. To circumvent this, you can put a limit order TO BUY with your online broker, saying that you want to purchase x number of shares at a price of £400 or below. If it hits that level the shares will be automatically purchased, if not, no harm is done.

This can be used on the flip side to lock in your upside/ limit your greed with an investment. If you were to buy a riskier asset like bitcoin, and decide that you want out when bitcoin hits £40,000, you can put your limit order TO SELL, and your investment will be sold at or above that price.

These are both useful ways of automating your buying and selling, so you can get in and out of your investment without the need for constant checking. Limit orders can also be set for a certain time period. If you want your limit order to last only a certain number of days, you can set it to auto-erase after this specified period, so you don't have to worry about forgetting to cancel it if it doesn't trigger.

Diversification

I was struggling to define diversification, so I looked it up. According to Google, diversification is the act of diversifying or becoming more diverse. Really helpful… The best way I can describe it is making sure that you don't put all your eggs in one basket, so that if one falls, you don't end up losing your 'nest egg.' It's an acknowledgement that we are not always right; not just because of human error or faulty decision making, but also because there are some things that are out of our control. Like the two examples I gave you earlier about China and Russia. Yes, I could have accounted for adverse 'geopolitical' events, but I could never have predicted those two things occurring. Or even COVID! Who could have predicted its occurrence and the huge impact on the markets? An impact that is still being felt today. What I want to cover is how to be truly diversified, along multiple asset classes, so you're not fooling yourself into thinking that you are.

When I was working as an Oral and Maxillofacial surgeon, I will never forget what a colleague said to me, let's call him Dr X. We were discussing an investment thesis around investing in gold. He had invested in gold mining companies. He told me he was well diversified, as he had invested in fifteen different mining companies. I cannot begin to tell you how much is wrong with this statement. Let's look at it like this, all it takes is the price of gold to drop. This one event would result in a significant reduction in the miners' profits, and his whole portfolio would drop. Gold mining companies have a low operating profit margin (due to the high costs of metal extraction), hence their profits fluctuate hugely when the price of gold increases.[1] Another factor that can have an impact is the price of the US dollar. The dollar and the price of gold move inversely to one another (when one goes up the other one goes down and vice versa). This happens as people move their money to gold as a safe haven. When the dollar is down, people go to gold, as a store of value. When the dollar price is increasing,

---

1   If it costs £2 to extract £3 of gold, they have a 50% margin (£3-£2/£2). If the price of gold increases twofold to £6, then their margin would increase fivefold (£6-£2/£2). Gold miners' profits proportionally increase more than the price of gold. The same is true when gold prices fall. They are often seen as a way to leverage gold.

people want to capitalise on this, so they move their money from gold into equities etc. These tendencies mean that any event that causes the dollar to rise, of which there are many, may cause gold to drop. Dr X's whole portfolio hinges on the price of gold! Let's hope the alchemists' society doesn't leak its secret recipe.

The main thing that is wrong with Dr X's statement is that he is only invested in one single asset class, precious metals. If the precious metals asset class underperform, his entire portfolio will underperform, no matter how good he is at finding mining stocks. Secondly, he has only invested in mining companies. Many mining companies are situated in areas with high geopolitical risk. When I asked what countries his mines were in, he said Canada, Uzbekistan, Peru, Ghana and Russia. Four of these countries undoubtedly carry the aforementioned geopolitical risk. On the plus side, at least his mines are diversified across five different countries. So, if Russia decides to invade Uzbekistan too, at least only his mines in the four other countries will continue to yield. If he wanted to bet everything on gold, then how could he have diversified better. I'm sure you know the answer by now… Dr X could have bought a gold ETF! Because if he hasn't picked well, his hand-selected fifteen miners could underperform even if gold increases! Even if gold quadruples in price, if his mines get flooded, if the government imposes sanctions, or the gold runs out, then those mining companies will suffer and bring down his portfolio. Now Dr X might have picked good miners, the price of gold could increase, leading to a big gain. However, what he definitely is not is well diversified.

To be truly diversified you have to spread your investments across multiple asset classes. These can be ETFs, stocks, bonds, real estate, commodities and cash/cash-equivalents. You can diversify within each individual asset class as well. For commodities, investing in oil, copper, lumbar as well as gold is wise. Commodities as a class tend to move together, but diversifying means if one of those assets are disproportionally affected, you don't miss out on a bullish run. Surprise surprise, there is an ETF for commodities.

If you want to diversify your stock selection, then invest in different sectors of business. If all your stocks are in technology stocks, if an event like the dot-com bust occurs, it will affect all tech stocks. It's good when they move up, but when they don't your portfolio will suffer. Look at a famous fund called ARK Innovation ETF. This fund was created by Cathie Wood, who went long on tech stocks. She was hailed one of the great investors of her time, with her ETF that is full of tech stocks. The stocks are varied, but in only one asset class. Often stocks in an asset class move together. Cathie Wood had huge success during the technology bull run; however, now, the average dollar invested in the fund has lost money.[1] I mentioned that asset classes and sectors tend to move together. Let's see how ARK Innovation fund matches up with the NASDAQ, the index for technology stocks. In Figure 9:6, you can see the similarities. While they are not the exact same, you can spot the same bull run starting in 2020, followed by the decline in 2022.

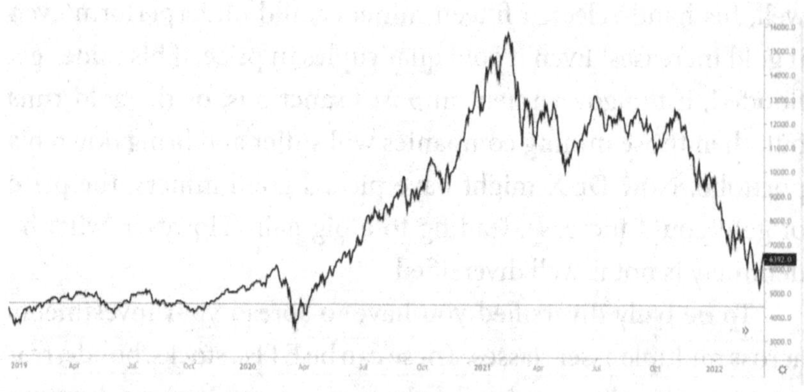

---

1 Cathie Wood isn't too worried, she has become incredibly rich with all the commissions she receives when people buy into her fund.

Figure 9:6: Share price of the ARK Innovation ETF (previous page) and the NASDAQ (above)

Another easy way to diversify is to invest in assets spanning multiple countries. Having all your money tied up in one country might be risky, even if it's a 'safe' country like the UK. Look at the effect Brexit (another event no one predicted) has had on the economy. It caused a 10% drop in the pound sterling (if you are only invested in one country, then you want to pick the biggest market, the US). The stocks I own are situated in the UK, US, Canada and China.

Diversification is like going to a roulette table and placing multiple bets with the hope that a few of them or one risky bet pays off big (like when you bet on a single number). You may find the more you diversify past a certain point, the more your winnings are diluted. For example, if you are from the future and know which stock will do well, then please, mortgage your house, sell a kidney and do not diversify! As you want to put as much of your money into the winning stock. Same as the roulette table, if by some divine miracle you know that the ball will land on 26 black, then it would be foolish to spread your money on black, even, 20-30 and on the single tile 26. Just put it all on 26 black and enjoy multiplying your net worth by thirty-five. When Carl Jung

139

was asked whether he believed in God, he replied: "I don't need to believe, I know." We can't all be Carl Jung, and we don't know which of our ideas will work, and we acknowledge this. Hence, we use diversification to make multiple bets, and in doing so reduce our risk. I'll leave you with a fascinating example. There were a group of Russian hackers who gained access to SEC's annual and quarterly reports before they were released to the public. This meant they knew exactly how well or badly a company did every quarter and year before the public did. This is called 'insider trading,' trading a company's stock with confidential, non-public information. This is a criminal offence which can carry a maximum sentence of twenty years in prison. One of the traders, named Irzak, 'insider traded' 150 companies, making millions of dollars. Having known exactly how the company performed before everyone else, you'd expect him to be like our hypothetical guy from the future, and get at least 95% of his trades correct. The most insane thing is that his success rate was only 66%! This man had all the answers and still won only 66% of the time. Bear in mind this man was no idiot; he was clever enough to hack the SEC! If this is not enough evidence to make you want to diversify, then I don't know what is. My advice to anyone out there planning on visiting the future is to remember lottery numbers instead. The SEC don't go after insider lottery winners…

Chapter 10
Growth Investing

Are you a value or a growth investor?

I don't personally like the terms value or growth investing, but it's a question I get asked a lot, and it's something you will definitely hear. The reason I don't like the terms being separated, is that good value and growth are not mutually exclusive, you can get both when you invest!

To explain the terms, value investing is finding stocks that are undervalued relative to their intrinsic value. In other words, investing in a company that is trading at a discount. Growth investing is investing in stocks with a higher growth potential. These normally trade at a higher price to earnings multiples, as future growth is anticipated and baked into the share price. Because of this, the investor will pay a higher price for this expected growth. If the company doesn't hit the expected growth, then investors may re-evaluate the share price to reflect the lower growth rate, causing a reduction in share price. The skill is evaluating price implied expectations. This refers to the expectations that are reflected by the price of the stock. A stock with a higher growth expectation, will have a higher priced stock relative to underlying earnings. The skill of the investor is analysing whether the expectations the market has placed on the company is accurate. If it isn't, is the market's estimation conservative, in which case selling at a discount to future growth. Or is it excessive, meaning the market is exceedingly optimistic. If you are investing in a company which has exceedingly optimistic valuations, then the company has to at least meet or outperform these future growth rates for a rise in share price. If the company falls short of these earnings, then a decline in price may materialise. If a company has a lower expected growth rate, and a higher growth rate materialises, then upward movement of the share price can be expected.

One company that has been mentioned before is Tesla. Let's have a look at the historical share prices and P/E ratios. As mentioned in the last section, P/E ratios are not the most accurate way to calculate earnings due to the potential for manipulation of earnings; however, we will use that ratio in this example. If you look at Tesla's earnings on the income statement, you will find they are quite similar to the cash flow statement of earnings, which means using the P/E ratio in this circumstance is acceptable.

Tesla has a growing revenue of 49.5% year over year taken over the last five years. This is the fastest growing car company, which greatly exceeds the other big car manufacturers. However, what is a realistic expectation for future growth? On 31 March 2022, Tesla's share price was $359, at a P/E ratio of 146. To compare it to a leading car manufacturer, Volkswagen's share price was at a P/E of 4.5 and an annual growth of 7.5% year over year for the last five years. When considering an investment in Tesla, the calculation you would have to make is whether at 146 times its earnings, is Tesla a good buy? For me this would have been too overvalued, as I didn't see the 49.5% growth as being sustainable. Currently the share price is around $170, at a P/E of 50. This is definitely more reasonable; however, still too high-priced for me to buy.

This isn't to say that investing in companies with high P/E

ratios is doomed to fail. This is far from the truth. Amazon in 2012 had a P/E ratio of 242, at a price of around $11. The chart of Amazon which I have included below was on a steady increase until 2022. Currently, midway through 2023, Amazon is trading at a P/E of 246. In the last five years the P/E has ranged from a minimum of 41 to a maximum of 261. As a value investor, a P/E of 246 is very high. However, if one had said that in 2012 and not invested in Amazon, then they would have missed out on the investing opportunity of a lifetime. They would have made seventy-eight times their initial investment. Amazon has shown incredible growth, justifying the higher than average P/E. However, what needs to be considered is that in 2012, the growth potential for Amazon was much greater, as they were not dominating the market like they are now. In 2012 they had much more room to grow, whereas now they already own a significantly larger market share. Market share refers to the total amount of industry sales that go to a company. For example, the leading automobile company in terms of market share statistics is Toyota. They own a market share of 11.5%. This means that of all the automobile sales in the world, 11.5% goes to Toyota. Obviously, this number changes depending on the company's success. However, the greater the market share a company occupies, the harder it is to increase. This is because market share is not infinite, so rival brands are competing for the same remaining market share, which becomes less and less the bigger a company gets.[1]

If we look at the S&P, the P/E ratio five-year average is 24.6, with it reaching as high as 39.9 in December 2020. The reason for the high in December was due to reduced earnings during COVID lockdowns.[2] While the price of the index did decrease,

---

1 This is why companies diversify into new sectors, as they may have growth potential in markets that they or another competitor hasn't saturated.

2 As P/E is the ratio of price to earnings. If the Earnings decrease, or Price increases, then the ratio will increase. So, the higher the P/E, the more 'expensive' a company is relative to its earnings.

it didn't decrease to the same extent as earnings. This is because earnings were expected to increase as the world reopened, so the market viewed it as a transient event. We may use the S&P P/E as an industry average of sorts, as the index makes up the largest 500 companies of the United States. We can use this as a guide to assess P/E multiples of other companies, and to evaluate the premium that the general market is valuing companies at. In a bull market, when more money is flowing into the market, P/E ratios will typically be higher than they are in a bear market. The premium that you wish to pay should be based on a comparison to other companies in the same sector, and the anticipated company growth rate. A company's historical or average P/E may also be used; however, if growth prospects change significantly, this value may be misleading.

My personal view surrounding companies trading at high price to earnings multiples is one of caution. I have been burnt many times by paying excessively for what we might call 'growth stocks.' It very much depends on the market conditions as mentioned earlier. If investing in a general bull market, higher valuations are acceptable, as market sentiment is higher and stock valuations are higher. In a bear market, a correction occurs which sends these valuations back to earth. When investing in growth stocks, I don't just look at the P/E as that would be a mistake. I look at the trends in income and growth rate, as well as a company's provisions to sustain future growth. In general, these growth stocks bring with them a higher risk, thus are placed within my higher risk portfolio. I will traditionally allocate a smaller percentage of my portfolio to these higher-risk investments. Some of my investments don't have a P/E ratio, as they haven't made a profit as of yet. Tesla didn't start making a profit until 2020! I look at these companies when wanting to invest in disruptive technology and innovations. I was recently researching a company involved in the technology for self-driving cars. I do believe in the future of self-driving cars, so wanted to profit from any potential upside. After researching the company LAZR, I liked their product and the progress they had made. Their share price was quite high, however, as it was based on their optimistic projected growth. Goldman Sachs had just downgraded them from neutral to sell, causing a share price drop of 10%. As a contrarian investor, I saw this as a potential buying opportunity. However, on evaluation, I felt the growth prospects of this company were limited, the worsening macroeconomic environment with a tightening money supply (from increasing interest rates) does not help a company that isn't making a profit and needs money to fund its research and development costs. More importantly, I didn't know enough about the self-driving space to confidently invest in LAZR. The way I could have invested in this idea more sensibly was to buy an ETF. We talked about this earlier when looking at 3D printing, which has revolutionised my own medical field, and will change other industries too. Currently, China is modelling invasions of Taiwan, which is the leading producer of semiconductors. This is a major concern, as a supply shortage of semiconductors is bad for technology, especially for the company LAZR! If we could 3D print them instead, this would be much easier. There are a few 3D printing ETFs that have a diversified portfolio of companies that would make a profit if 3D printing became more universal. This is a way to diversify your investments and thus reduce risk.

Beware of ZOMBIES!

In the introduction I mention cyborgs, and now I am talking about zombies. You must think I'm strange… Believe it or not, zombie companies are actually a financial term. Zombie companies are ones that earn just enough to service their operating costs and debt interest payments, but do not make enough to pay off their debt or have any excess working capital. The lack of working capital means they cannot invest in the business to create growth. They are normally cash burning companies with a negative free cash flow (burning more cash than they earn). Zombies pop up during boom markets, when interest rates are low, money is flowing into the market, and borrowing is easier. When the cost of borrowing goes up, these companies can't service their debt repayments, leading to default and bankruptcy.

An example of such is ARK Innovation ETF led by Cathie Wood. This is an ETF focused on disruptive innovation. Cathie Wood started this fund in 2014, and since then has been hailed as a genius, with her ETF being called the 'new NASDAQ.' Her fund really picked up in 2020, which is when interest rates dropped to almost 0%, creating cheap money, increased lending and increased investment in the stock market, the fuel for the ensuing boom. This easy money went flying into this ETF, as these disruptive innovation technology stocks represented growth. The ETF soared more than 375%! When the government started tightening rates, making borrowing for these cash burning businesses difficult, the cracks started to show. The curtains fell, and the zombies were laid bare. The fund has lost more than 70% from its high, and the average dollar invested in the fund since inception has lost money.

This is not to say all businesses that don't make money can't become profitable, it's just a warning that comes with so-called growth investing. Make sure you avoid buying zombies when looking for a canary.

Chapter 11
Value Investing

Some of the most famous investors are value investors. Warren Buffett and his partner Charlie Munger are value investors. They learnt this style from the teachings of Benjamin Graham, known as the godfather of value investing. His book *The Intelligent Investor* is well worth a read. The focus of value investing is not just about the quality of a company, but about the price you pay for it. As a value investor we look to invest in a company that is trading at a discount to its intrinsic value. Its intrinsic value refers to the inherent value of a share. A share usually stays around its intrinsic value, but of course can deviate massively from this amount. This variation exists due to the variability and, to a degree, the uncertainty of how to calculate intrinsic value. In this lies the million-dollar question, how does one calculate intrinsic value?

There are many methods of calculating it, some of them get very complex. The common error in these calculations comes from assumptions of the future. Estimations of future revenue is exactly as the name suggests, an estimation. Below, I will outline three methods to calculate intrinsic value: Financial Metric method, Asset-Based valuation and Discounted Cash Flow. The first two we will discuss in detail. The latter is quite complex, so I will explain the main points, but will not dive deep into the mathematics.

Financial Metric Method

Calculation using financial metrics is one that uses Earning per share, P/E ratio and the expected rate of return. There are a few variations to this calculation, which we will cover. The formula is:

Intrinsic Value = Earnings Per Share x 1 (1 + Growth Rate) x Price Earnings ratio

In short form:

Intrinsic Value = EPS x (1 + GR) x P / E

1. **Earnings per share (EPS)**
   EPS is set and should only be adjusted if the earnings deviate significantly from the free cash flow (as discussed in Chapter 6).
2. **The Growth Rate**
   The growth rate is the expected annual rate of growth. This is a number which should be calculated with some caution. This can be simplified by taking the average growth for the past five years; however, it doesn't take into account changes in growth rate. This is where a qualitative analysis of a company's growth potential must be assessed. Based on this assessment, a decision can be made on whether the growth of the past is greater, lesser or an accurate figure to predict future growth.
   To calculate the growth rate, the compounded annual growth

rate (CAGR) should be used. If Company A grows by 50% in two years, its CAGR is **not** 50% divided by two. We have to take into account that after year 1, the company is now bigger. For year 2 to match year 1's growth rate, it needs to grow by more to make the same growth rate. The CAGR for Company A is in fact 22.5% for the two-year period. To go through the example, let's say Company A goes from £100 to £125 after year 1. Then from year 1 to year 2 it goes from £125 to £150. In both years it has grown by the same raw amount of £25. However, in year 1 it grew by 25% (25/100) and in year 2 by 20% (25/125). Hence why the CAGR equals 22.5%, which lies in between the two figures. The easiest way to calculate this is by typing into Google 'CAGR calculator.' You simply need to input the starting value, the end value, and the number of years apart. You can get these values of earnings going back more than ten years from a website called Macrotrends.

3. **The P/E Ratio**

The P/E ratio can be set as the average for the company, the average for the sector or an arbitrary number used by the investor. I prefer the latter, selecting my arbitrary P/E depending on what sector I am investing in. For example, for the technology sector I will select a higher P/E number than if I was evaluating a company in the commodity sector. For this example, we will use the lowest P/E for the last five years. By using the lowest P/E, our intrinsic value calculation will be more conservative. Let's look at Apple:

APPLE Intrinsic Value Calculation

EPS – $5.89

GR – 8.02% per annum for next five years (taken from Yahoo Finance estimated growth)

P/E – 12.4 – the lowest P/E for the last five years (taken from Macrotrends)

$$\text{Intrinsic Value with a one-year forecast} = \$5.89 \times (1 + 0.0802) \times 12.4 = \$78.89 \text{ per share}$$

We must now compare this to the current value of Apple, which is trading at $173.56 per share. This simplified calculation would suggest that Apple stock is **overvalued** if the stock market priced its stock with only a one-year forecast period. In reality, the market is about five years forward-looking, even though it tends to overreact to short-term factors. If we want to get an estimation of the current day prices that the market sets, we need to be forward-looking for about five years in our calculation. To do so we would look at multiplying the GR by a power of five:

$$\text{Intrinsic Value with a 5-year forecast} = \$5.89 \times (1 + 0.0802)^5 \times 12.4 = \$107.41 \text{ per share?}$$

One factor we have not considered is the returns the shareholder gets from dividend payments. Apple doesn't pay the best of dividends, only paying 0.55%. (Strictly speaking, the investors are taxed for these payments so this should be deducted from the 0.55% but we will omit this.) If we include this in the return:

$$\text{Intrinsic Value including dividend} = 5.89 \times (1 + 0.0802 + 0.0055)^5 \times 12.4 = \$137.68 \text{ per share?}$$

Looking at this calculation, it suggests that the Apple stock is overvalued, meaning that it would not be considered for a buy based on our calculations. We have to bear in mind, however, that the greater into the future we try and forecast, the greater our error. For example, what if Apple increase their dividend to 2%, or what if growth drops to half because Samsung release a revolutionary phone? For these reasons, we need to include a margin of error in our calculation. If we give a margin of safety of 20% of the estimated value, this brings our calculation to:

Estimated Intrinsic Value x (1 – Margin Safety) = $137.68 x (1 – 0.2) = $110.14

With the margin of safety calculation, our intrinsic value calculation is very far from Apple's current stock price. The reason being, that investors at this current time are willing to pay a much higher P/E valuation for the privilege of owning Apple.

If we did the above intrinsic value calculation using Apple's average P/E (instead of its lowest P/E) for the last five years of 24.6 (taken from YCharts), then we get an intrinsic value with a 20% margin of safety equal to $174.86. This is very close to the current stock price of $173.56. All of these calculations lead us to the decision of whether or not to buy or sell the stock. The questions I ask myself are:

1. How undervalued is the intrinsic value compared to the current value? – This will determine the magnitude of the return.
2. How confident am I with the company's rate of growth? – This will determine the risk of the investment.
3. How much of a margin of safety do I have with these calculations? – As above, this will affect the risk of the investment.

4. What opportunity is there of other investment modalities that may offer better returns and/or the same return with lower risk?

It comes down to a risk–reward calculation. Taking a higher risk should offer the possibility of a higher reward. See the risk as the fee for the opportunity to increase the rate of return. The amount of risk you wish to take on an investment is down to you as the investor. As mentioned before, I have a lower- and higher-risk portfolio, so that I can compartmentalise my decision making. I limit the amount in my higher-risk portfolio, as I naturally have a higher risk tolerance, thus want to limit this.

The last question we address when buying a stock is what opportunities are offered by other stocks? This comes to what we call the cost of capital, or opportunity cost. Whenever we put money into an investment, we need to consider the returns we can achieve without any risk. No investment is risk-free, but the closest is bonds backed by the government. Usually, you will see the US government using T-bills, which we discussed in the section on bonds. Some people use triple AAA-rated corporate bonds, though these are riskier than the government ones. Well, depending on the government…

The US thirty-year T-bill is at 3.8%. To factor this in:

$$Intrinsic\ Value\ with\ cost\ of\ capital = \frac{Intrinsic\ Value}{(1 + bond\ rate)^5}$$

$$Intrinsic\ Value\ with\ cost\ of\ capital = \frac{\$137.68}{(1 + 0.038)^5} = \$114.26$$

As you can see, there are lots of variables one can add into the equation.

1. The first is growth rate. We can use growth rate from past growth, expected future growth from the annual statement, predicted growth from investment sites like Yahoo Finance, or our own expectations of growth.
2. For P/E ratio, we can use the average for the company, average for the sector, or a base P/E you personally are willing to pay for a company or sector.
3. The forecast time can be adjusted. Some share prices reflect growth that is more forward-looking than others, so five years may be too long to estimate the value of a company, especially if it's a riskier company.
4. The margin of safety can vary depending on the confidence in the aforementioned factors, or your own personal risk tolerance.
5. The cost of capital calculation can vary depending on the benchmark utilised, be it government bonds or AAA corporate bonds.

All the variables mentioned above result in wide variations in intrinsic value calculations. As we have seen above, switching the P/E from the five-year low to the five-year average results in calculations of $110 versus $174. All these potential variants are what lead to the fluctuation of stock prices. This is the basis behind value investing. Finding companies whose market value, aka the general public's appraisal of intrinsic value, is less than the investors' calculation of intrinsic value.

Asset-Based

Asset based is as the name suggests, based on the assets owned by the company. This method of intrinsic value calculation gives us the 'book value' of a company. Its book value as mentioned before in Chapter 6, is a company's total assets minus its liabilities. It doesn't take into account whether these assets generate any income. It also doesn't account for misrepresentation of what is and what isn't an asset, which is often inflated to increase the 'book value'. I would only use this to calculate intrinsic values for companies, whose value comes principally from ownership of said assets. An example is a REIT – Real Estate Investment Trust. These are companies that own properties. Investors can buy shares of these trusts, essentially becoming an owner of the properties included in this trust. You can appreciate how valuing this company on its assets may be useful. If I was to do this analysis, I would comb through the balance sheet as we did in Chapter 6, removing any items I didn't want included in the calculations. To calculate this, we subtract the Total Assets away from the Total Liabilities.[1]

Intrinsic value = Total Assets - Total liabilities

The other time this may be useful is for companies going into default (bankruptcy). This company no longer generates income and is looking at selling its assets. These assets then get distributed to the debtors (including bondholders) and shareholders. The bankruptcy value is normally nowhere near the book value. Firstly, because some assets are listed as more than their actual worth. And secondly, because certain things that held value

---

1 Footnote- Bear in mind that the value of bonds issued should be included as a liability, as they are owed money. Bonds are normally included in the liability section of a company's balance sheet.

when the company was operational, no longer has any value. Inventories for example, aren't worth anything near like they are when the company is functional.

Distressed investing is buying companies that are teetering on bankruptcy. The strategy is to find distressed companies that are selling at less than their liquidation value. However, calculating their liquidation value is tough, as you have to be able to estimate the true value of the assets in the balance sheets. Benjamin Graham suggested an easy way to calculate liquidation value. He ignores the non-current assets, using only the current assets and subtracting them by total liabilities.

Intrinsic value (in bankruptcy) = Total Current Assets - Total Liabilities

NB – If you are looking to buy the company's bonds, then you do not need to include the Bond holders' value as a liability. If you are a shareholder, calculating what you will receive in liquidation, you will need to subtract any shares that have a priority over your shares (see Chapter 1).

For investing in distressed debt (see Chapter 2), an investor can find companies that can be close to bankruptcy, but recover enough to pay their bondholders in full. Distressed investing is a real skill, that can bring excellent returns. However, it is a high risk strategy and is extremely difficult to do. I do not dabble in this field, due to lack of expertise in the area rather than lack of want.

Discounted Cash Flow

The discounted cash flow (DCF) method uses a lot of what we discussed in the financial metric method, putting them all together in a more complex formula. It uses free cash flows (FCFs), expected future FCFs, cost of capital, current cash holdings and cash equivalents minus debts. In this way it combines aspects of the financial metric and the asset-based methods of valuation discussed earlier. Note that it uses free cash flows and not earnings, as FCFs are true and not manipulated figures. The 'discounted' part in the name is because it discounts future cash to present value, taking into consideration that £1 today will be worth less in one year, as this money could be invested and so forth. To summarise, it calculates in the present day what the value of the cash holdings of a business (in excess of debts), and the future cash generation of the company, is worth to the shareholders.

1. **Free cash flows and future growth**
   Current free cash flow of a company is used, which is then amplified by a predicted rate of growth, giving us the expected future cash flows. The rate of growth is normally estimated over a five-year period, in which growth is then assumed to slow down to what it calls terminal growth. This growth is more in line with the average of an industry. It's not saying that growth will stop in five years; it's simply stating that this is the longest period they are willing to forecast at the given estimated growth rate.

2. **Cost of capital**
   It then calculates the cost of this growth, called the WACC, or the Weighted Average Cost of Capital. This calculates how much a company has to pay its debt holders, and how much it pays its shareholders. It deducts this from the FCF and future FCFs.

3. **Enterprise value**
   They add the total number of years of cash flow generation, arriving at the enterprise value. This represents the future cash flow of the business with predicted growth. The next step is adding the cash and cash equivalent (as we covered

when going through balance sheets), and subtracting debt.

4. **Intrinsic value calculation**

They add this all together, divide it by the total number of shares and arrive at the DCF value per share. You can then compare this value to the share price, and see if the share price is overvalued, undervalued or accurate. In this calculation we can use a margin of safety as used above.

When doing a DCF analysis on Apple using the same numbers for growth as seen above, I arrived at a figure of $112.79. This is similar to our calculations above using financial metrics when factoring in the cost of capital. Using both the financial metric-based and the DCF calculations, the large difference between the calculated intrinsic value and the share price means the stock is **overvalued**, and isn't a stock that I would consider buying at the current predicted growth rates. This could change if a new development arises, for example, one which significantly increases the predicted growth rate.

For argument's sake let's say that we had used a higher P/E to make our calculations and achieved an intrinsic value calculation for Apple equal to $210 per share. This would have been above the current share price of $173.56, meaning the stock price is **undervalued** relative to its intrinsic value. Whether or not this is a buying opportunity would all depend on the factors discussed above. Have we factored in a margin of safety? If we were to add a 20% margin of safety then it brings our intrinsic value calculation to $168. How confident are we of the predicted growth rate, and is it sustainable? What other opportunities are out there which may serve as a better investment?

Contrarian Investing

A strategy that helps me find value opportunities is contrarian investing. Contrarian investing is going against the general trend. This can be selling when people are buying, or buying when people are selling. In Chapter 8 we discussed market cycles. Being a contrarian means getting in at the beginning of the cycle, earlier than the crowd. In booms and busts, which represent the extreme ends of a market cycle, investors behave erratically. At the height of a bubble, investors disregard price and invest in high-risk ventures, being of the belief that 'the only way for the market is up.' At times of busts, investors lose faith in the market, believing that the risk is too great, giving up opportunities to pay heavily discounted rates for stocks because of the belief that there is no money to be made in the market. As Warren Buffett said: "The less prudence with which others conduct their affairs, the greater prudence with which we should conduct our own affairs." The same goes the other way round, when investors are terrified of the market, the more we should look to capitalise.

In general, the market tends to be forward-looking and take a long-term view. However, in the short term it is prone to overreaction and irrational behaviour. Benjamin Graham called the market Mr Market, saying that Mr Market has Manic-Depressive characteristics. Mr Market is emotional, going from periods of euphoria to lows, and is irrational. One of his famous quotes is that the market "in the short run is a voting machine, but in the long run a weighing machine." This is similar to what was mentioned above, that it overreacts in the short term, but corrects itself in the long term.

I love to see overreactions of the market and take advantage of this. The thing to be wary of are value traps. Value traps are stocks that on examination have a stock price that appears to be trading at a significant discount, and typically very low valuation metrics. Such as low price to earnings, price to cash flow and price to book value. However, these companies are not trading at as good a value as it seems, due to factors unforeseen by the investor. We will go through some examples of contrarian investing from my own portfolio.

A good example of value opportunities is the COVID lockdowns. The general market dropped significantly, including most of the blue-chip stocks. We examine in depth two value plays during this period in Chapter 17. Another in particular that caught my eye was McDonald's. During the closures in lockdown revenue got slammed, the stock market reacted accordingly, with a large downward move, moving the share price from trading at $215 a share to $170 a share. At this price, I saw a 20% drop as an overreaction to closures which I believed at the time were temporary. My plan was to buy the share and hold it until the world reopened and McDonald's revenues returned to pre-COVID levels.

As it happens, the stock dropped a further 15% to $145 where it bottomed. The reason I included this example is that it shows the risk of contrarian investing. Getting in too early brings the risk of being hit with more downside. I was happy to pay $170 for the stock at the time and had a long-term outlook, so I had no obligation to sell and realise losses if the stock fell further in price. What may have been more prudent would have been to wait for the market to show signs of an uptrend before buying a stock, which has just experienced a recent sell-off. If I had waited for an uptrend to materialise, I would have seen the stock drop to $145, detected the start of an uptrend and picked up the stock for less than $170, realising a greater gain.

One example of getting in too early was Alibaba (the Chinese version of Amazon). The disappearance of Jack Ma, the CEO of Alibaba, caused concern among foreign investors. This happened after he made comments criticising the Chinese Communist Party's leadership. China also blocked Jack Ma's new IPO release, and created antitrust regulations that negatively affected Alibaba. It made investors concerned from a geopolitical standpoint.

So, due to the macroeconomic headwinds, the stock dropped. I bought what I thought was trading at a huge discount. The stock had decreased from $300 a share to $180, a 40% decrease. At this price point, I decided to buy, without doing my proper due diligence with regards to intrinsic value calculation. I ended up severely overpaying for the stock at $180; it spiralled further down to $85. In this scenario, as above, I would have benefited from waiting for an uptrend, before getting in too early.

The last example we will go over is Carnival. This is one of the biggest cruise ship companies, which took a big financial hit during COVID. Their price tanked from $45 to $7. Unlike McDonald's, the travel industry took much longer to rebound due to fears of going abroad, hassles of quarantining, testing etc. With cruise shipping in particular, involving lots of people stuck on a boat, I predicted this would take the longest to recover. Carnival had huge amounts of debt, and needed to take on more debt to prevent insolvency (going bankrupt). At $7, however, the company was 'cheap', trading at 57% of its book value.[1] Due to the high debt levels and no signs of near-term recovery of the cruising industry, I decided that at $7 it was a value trap. As it happens had you bought it at that price and held it for a year, you would have earned around 250–300% on your investment. Currently it is trading at $13, so you still would have made nearly double your money. I still believe it is not a buy, as the company is not making a profit and the debt is still too high. Right now, we are in a period where interest rates are rising, and the cost of

---

1 If you remember from earlier in the chapter, book value is a poor measure of a company's liquidation value. However, trading at low valuation metrics, such as a price to book value of 0.56, is a classic sign of potential value traps.

debt is increasing. If we recall from Chapter 8 where we discussed the credit cycle, this is the contraction of credit. When Carnival goes to refinance its debts, it may not be able to do so. If it does, it will do so at a higher interest rate, putting more strain on the business.

Chapter 12
Indexing and ETFs

Indexing is a passive investment strategy that aims to give the investor returns equal to the general performance of a sector. We discussed indices such as the S&P 500, FTSE and the NASDAQ in Chapter 3. If we wanted to capture the general gains of the market, we would look to invest in an index fund. This is the ultimate form of diversification, which is something we looked at in Chapter 9. The return from indexing represents the returns of the market as a whole. Everyone wants to try and pick the best stocks, and theoretically, it will give you a much higher return if you manage to pick the correct ones. Therein lies the crux, that you have to be good at picking the best ones. In a study comparing returns of private equity funds (that have managers that actively pick stocks), with the returns of the S&P 500 (representing the passive return of the market), then for the last fifteen years, only 7% of equity funds beat the market. So not only do most hedge funds charge a premium to manage your money, but they also deliver inferior returns in the long run. It tells you the power of indexing. It allows diversification, reduction of risk and gives a predictable result in the long run. The best way to index is to 'dollar cost average.'

Dollar Cost Averaging

Dollar cost averaging (DCA) is the method of passive investing, which involves investing equal amounts of money at set intervals. The investor does NOT try to time the market, aka try to buy low and sell high. The whole theory behind DCA is that the investor is trying to capture the general move of the market, eliminating the volatility that comes with it. As sometimes you will buy on a dip, and sometimes you will buy on a high, but in general your returns will be aligned with the average market return. When people refer to DCA, they will talk about using it for index fund investing (indexing), though theoretically, you can DCA anything. I spoke to an investor recently (or should I say 'crypto bro') that told me he was dollar cost averaging bitcoin…

If we compare the returns of DCA versus one lump sum investment, we will see how much timing plays a role if we chose not to DCA. The study compares two methods, one that DCA and one that invests as a lump sum. The start date was January 2007, the DCA method invested the amount spread out monthly until January 2021, whereas the lump sum put the whole amount in 2007. They used the SDPR S&P index tracking fund.[1] Bear in mind that a large market crash occurred in 2009.

DCA from 2007 to 2021 gives a return over that period of 360%, with a maximum drawdown of -17.7% (refers to the lowest the portfolio reached in the times between 2007 and 2021). The person who lump sum invested for the same period got an appreciation of 300% with a maximum drawdown of -48.6%. While both investors made money, you can see that the person who invested lump sum not only achieved lower returns, but also experienced more volatility, as the drawdown was -48.6% vs

---

1   If you remember from Chapter 3, you can't invest directly into an index, you need to use a tracking ETF known as an index fund.

the -17.7% for the DCA. For the lump sum investor, timing is everything. This is not what indexing and hence passive investing is about. To give you an example of how timing can affect returns, if you had invested right at the peak of the market, before the crash in 2009, you would have returned 280%, with a maximum drawdown of -52.2%. If, however, you had been lucky enough, or 'genius' enough, to invest at the market bottom in March 2009, you would have returned 580% with no drawdown (as you invested at the bottom). I'm sure this higher return of 580% is enticing; however, this relies on perfect timing. The market is very unpredictable, and not easy to time. This is where the magic of DCA comes in. It eliminates this need to time the market.

ETFs

This far into the book I'm sure you know what an ETF is. It is a basket of stocks aimed to increase diversification for an investor. Anyone can make an ETF, you just have to put marketable securities together and sell them. Currently there are more than 8,000 ETFs, managing in total about 10 trillion dollars. One of the main reasons for writing this book was the number of people who gave their money to active managers, who were not actively managing, but just buying ETFs for their clients. In effect you are paying them commission, to pay the ETF manager's commission. Why not just buy the ETFs yourself? That way you only pay one management fee. ETFs are a great way to capture a strategy or specific sector, maintain diversification, while being more concentrated and targeted than if you were to invest in an index.

I'll give an example of an ETF I purchased using a top-down approach. With inflation and a potential recession, I wanted to pick companies that would still thrive despite these macroeconomic headwinds. Given the recent war in Russia and

Ukraine, China threating to take over Taiwan, one thing countries will not be stingy on is spending on defence. The US in particular are big spenders. They spend the most in the world, forking out three times more than China, who are the second biggest defence spenders. An ETF I recently bought to capture this was the iShares U.S. Aerospace & Defense fund. Alternatively, I could have done a deep dive into the accounts of defence stocks and tried to pick the best ones. As I know nothing about how the US government picks defence companies, or in fact how a country defends itself, I thought it better to diversify my portfolio with an ETF.

Chapter 13
Fixed Income Investing

The way I explain fixed income investing, is the stock market's version of a 'buy to let' approach. 'Buy to let' in the property world is buying, leasing, and profiting from the rental income. Fixed income investing is like this in a way. It's buying a security, to earn a figure which is a percentage of the initial investment. The examples we will cover are investing for stock dividends and purchasing of bonds.

Bonds

Bonds have a set coupon rate, which determines the return you get. Bond investing has been made a lot easier with the credit rating systems provided by multiple companies. The three main ones I recommend using are, Moody's, Standard and Poor's (S&P) and Fitch Ratings. They grade investments from AAA to D. There are two categories, Investment grade or Junk bonds. Investment grade goes from AAA to BBB-. Anything below BBB- is considered junk, this is BB+ to D. Traditionally the lower the rating, the higher the coupon, thus the higher the yield. This is the compensation for taking on more risk. In addition, the bond may be selling at a discount to par (original) value. If you hold the bond till maturity, then a profit can be made when the company pays back the bondholder at the starting par value. If you sell before maturity, you will receive whatever the market rate is, which may be at par, higher than or lower than par. Using these ratings, you can decide how much risk you want to take on, and what return you want to receive.

If you want to take on more risk, then the lower rated junk bonds provide higher returns but higher risk. We talked about distressed bonds investing and the risks that come with this in Chapter 2. The most important thing to evaluate with bond investing is the company's ability to pay back its bondholders' interest payments. At maturity, the company also has to be able to pay off the par value of the bonds it issued. This may be a substantial amount, which a company does not necessarily have in cash or cash equivalents. It can seek refinancing to pay the bondholders their premiums.

Below we cover how to evaluate a company's ability to pay a stock dividend by calculating the dividend cover, we can also apply the same principle to bonds. However, do not take tax payments into consideration for bond calculations. This is because debt/bond payments are made from pre-tax income. This is in contrast to dividend payments, which are made from post-tax income.

Stock Dividends

Companies which pay higher dividends tend not to be our typical 'growth' stocks. We also talked about how the blue-chip stocks have taken to not paying out much or any dividend. In Chapter 10 we looked at Apple, which is a company that gushes free cash, but only pays a 0.55% dividend! There are plenty of companies out there that do pay a healthy dividend.

To go through what I look for when buying a stock for a dividend:

1. **Dividend history**

    I look back to the last twenty years, and see how many times the company hasn't paid a dividend, and how many times they have reduced their dividend payout.

2. **Dividend yield**

    I look at the yield of the dividend; for stock investing I won't accept less than 5%, and I like to see a historical dividend which has been increasing over time.

3. **Dividend Cover**

    This assesses whether the earnings of the company are sufficient to sustain the dividend payments. When examining the cash flow statement, I assess the cash flow after all operating expenses have been paid, and see whether the dividend payment is sustainable (see Chapter 6).

    NB – For Bonds, I don't deduct tax-related expenses, as the interest payments can be made pre-tax.

4. **Fairly priced company**

    Fairly priced company relative to its intrinsic value.

Let's look at a company I bought recently for fixed income investing. The company is called Legal & General, which is an insurance company.

1. **Dividend History**

    Dividend history (type in dividend history with company name and it will come up)

    A steady increase in dividends, with no missed payments, and only one reduction in payment during the 2009 crash going back twenty years. I have included the nine-year chart below. As you can see, they increased every year apart from 2020 (COVID year) where they kept it the same.

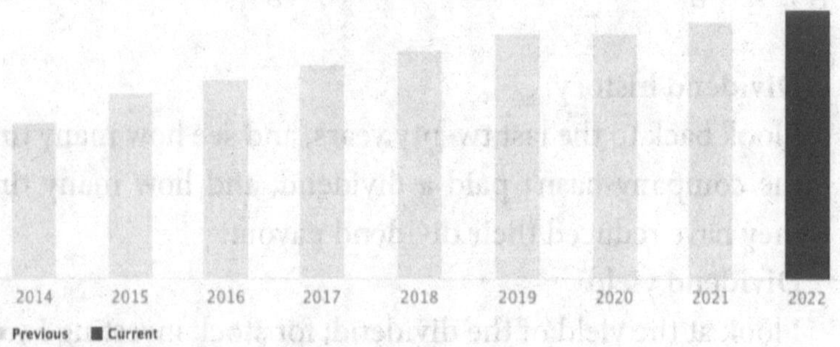

Figure 13:1: Legal & General – Dividends.

2. **Dividend yield**
    8.21%. This is a more than satisfactory yield

3. **Dividend cover**
    The company's net cash flow from operations in 2022 was $20.5 billion, whereas the dividend payment was just over $1 billion. This means the dividend is only 5% of the company's cash flow, which is more than sustainable.

4. **Fair share price relative to intrinsic value**
    The fair price calculation I achieved was 363.97p. At a current price of 235.20p I am happy that it is trading at below its intrinsic worth.

After analysing the company, I decided it was a good fixed income investment opportunity, and bought it for my dividend portfolio.

TASK – Do the same analysis with a company called 3M (ticker symbol – MMM). Let's see what conclusion you come to with this company.

Chapter 14

Cryptocurrency – Volatility vs Fundamentals

I included this small chapter in the book because it is such a hot topic it's hard to ignore. I have an extremely small portion of my portfolio in cryptocurrency and I will cover why. I won't delve deep into cryptocurrency for two reasons: firstly, because I don't know that much about it, and secondly, because it doesn't interest me that much. There are, however, some interesting talking points that I will share.

When you invest in something you should always have a reason for doing so. This reason should be in line with your investing philosophy. By investing philosophy, I am referring to your beliefs, personality, investing style and risk tolerance. There are three principal reasons for people to invest in crypto. One of those reasons is its volatility, and the other two are based on its fundamentals.

Volatility

The volatility of an asset can be referred to as its beta. It's a reference of volatility compared to a big index such as the S&P. The S&P has a beta of one. Any beta lower than that is less volatile, and any higher is more volatile. The more volatile the asset, the higher the beta and thus the higher the risk. With more risk brings more reward.

Cryptocurrency has huge amounts of volatility, in which great gains and losses can materialise. In the past month, it has gone from £16k to £25k, showing a 56% gain. It is still 50% lower than its all-time high. One strategy is to try to capture any upside, harnessing this volatility. At what point you decide to buy is based on your prediction of whether you think the price is going to increase. You can't base this on intrinsic value, as crypto has no inherent intrinsic value in the same way a share of a company does. So, you have to base it on the thoughts of the masses and/or signs from technical trading, which we will cover in Chapter 15. When buying for volatility, you have to make sure there is someone willing to pay a higher price for the asset; as when there isn't, you are going to be making a loss. You may think if the trade doesn't go your way, then you'll just hold it. But if you bought bitcoin at £40k, thinking there were no limits to it, and are sitting on a 38% loss, do you cut your losses, or do you hold? If you hold, then how long do you lock that money in for before you decide to sell? All difficult questions to which there are no easy answers. This is the reason I don't trade for volatility, as I want to have an answer to these questions to allow me to make rationale investment decisions.

Fundamentals

Investing for fundamentals is looking at the characteristics of an asset that make them desirable and give them worth. There are two fundamental reason one might want to own cryptocurrency. One is for store of value, the other is for what is known as 'tokenomics'.

Bitcoin is a decentralised currency. By decentralised, we refer to it not being controlled by the government. Unlike our currency, the government cannot decide to print more bitcoin, and its supply is limited. There are only a certain number of bitcoins that can exist due to the blockchain technology. It is an alternative to fiat currency. Previously, money was tied to a physical asset, gold. This preserved the value of money, as the government couldn't print more money than it held in gold. During the Great Depression of 1931, England needed to print more money to support the economy, resulting in a withdrawal from the gold standard. Nowadays, fiat money is not tied to any physical commodity; it is backed by the government. If we look at the current rate of inflation caused by rampant money printing, we can see the ability the government has to weaken a currency. Bitcoin, on the other hand, has a limited supply. Theoretically it is inflation-proof in this sense, as it can't just be printed. Like gold, it retains its value due to its scarcity.

In a 2011 letter to shareholders, Warren Buffett had this to say about gold:

> Gold ... has two significant shortcomings, being neither of much use nor procreative. True, gold has some industrial and decorative utility, but the demand for these purposes is both limited and incapable of soaking up new production. Meanwhile, if you own one ounce

of gold for an eternity, you will still own one ounce at its end.

While I agree with his assessment of gold utility, I disagree that these are shortcomings. In fact, I would argue that this is gold's greatest quality, that it's inert, shiny and does absolutely nothing. This is why it acts as a store of value! It has acted as a store of value for more than 500 years, and has held up against the test of time. For the last fifty-one years, gold has given an average annual return of 7.78%. For something that is supposedly 'doing nothing' it sure hasn't performed badly. One reason for its rise is the degradation of fiat currency. Due to money printing and inflation, cash holdings lose their inherent value relative to assets like gold. This is why gold acts as a store of value.

When bitcoin was undergoing its seemingly unstoppable bullish run, people were hailing it as the 'new gold.' It has limited supply, was decentralised from the government's abuse and was being used for transactions of goods. It was everything you might want for a store of value. This is the reason I currently own bitcoin, as a hedge to inflation and a store of value. Even though its properties make it a suitable store of value, it still behaves like a risk on volatile asset. This is not what one wants from a store of value. In fact, bitcoin moves in lockstep with the technology NASDAQ index. It is still trading like a 'risk on' asset, as it moves with tech stocks. When it decouples from this, and its price stabilises, then we may be able to call it a 'risk off' asset. I, however, would not compare it to gold by any means, as it has not passed the test of time like gold has. I have personally invested a very small amount, seeing it as a potential store of value. Time will tell whether I was correct in this theory.

The second reason is the tokenomics, or the economics of the tokens. Cryptocurrencies have properties which are very useful to the finance industry. They allow faster transactions, lower costs, better monitoring and many other things. They are undeniably very useful to a society where tech is an integral part of our lives. Many crypto investors delve deep into the workings of coins and invest based on their usability and functions. I don't know enough about tech, so I don't even try to understand the workings of some of the products out there.

One comment to make about the cryptocurrency space is that all the coins generally tend to move with bitcoin. If bitcoin falls, all the other cryptocurrencies fall. We should see bitcoin as the standard bearer, of sorts.

Cryptocurrency is a risky asset and should only make up a small part of your portfolio with money that you are willing to lose. By the time you read this, things may have changed. With ChatGPT, and AIs making songs for Drake without him singing a word, who knows what the future holds…

lower cost, better monitoring and many other things. They are undeniably expected to take a stake where it gets to injected part of our lives. Many crypto investors delve deep into the workings of coins and infer based out their results, and statements. I don't know enough about tech, so I don't even try to understand the workings around the products out there.

One mustn't to make about the cryptocurrency space is that all the coins generally tend to move with bitcoin. If bitcoin falls, all the other cryptocurrencies fall. We should see basing of the standard bitcoin altcoins.

Cryptocurrency is a risky asset and should only make up a small part of your portfolio with money that you are willing to lose. By the time you read this, things may have changed. Who had... had the making things for Dogecoin with joining a word when know what the future holds.

Chapter 15
Technical Trading

When I started my journey and blew my initial investment, it was from trying to technical trade. So this holds a special place in my heart (heavy sarcasm). On a serious note, I vowed to never technical trade again, and I have kept that promise. Let's go over what technical trading is.

Technical analysis, as it is otherwise known, is making investment decisions based on patterns and trends that exist in the market. They are of the belief that even random movements in price have identifiable patterns that can be predicted. They use price action, chart patterns, momentum indicators, moving averages, support and resistance levels and many others. This is in contrast with fundamental analysis, which is analysis of earnings, future prospects and intrinsic value.

It would take a whole book to cover technical analysis in sufficient depth, but I will cover a few examples here of technical indicators that you might hear or read about. To learn about it, I went on a course, which is a good way to get into it if it's something that you are interested in.

Candlestick Charts

Price action can be described as the way that the market price fluctuates. Analysing price action is a key component of technical analysis. Candlestick charts help give us information on the action of buyers (bulls) and sellers (bears) at a given timeframe. To understand candlestick charts, let's look at figure 15.1. There are two components, the wick (the long thin line) and the body (the rectangle box). The wick shows where the price of said security moved over the day. The body shows at what price the market opened, and at what price the market closed. If the market price went down during the day, then the box colour is red or black. If the price increases, then the box colour is white or green. On Figure 15.1, we can see that as the box is black, we know the price went down. The market opened at point A. it then fluctuated to point D and point C over the course of the day, then ended the day on point B. For a bullish candlestick (one where price increases over the day), the point A where the market opens would be at the bottom of the box, and the point B where the market closes would be at the top of the box (you can see this on figure 15.2)

If we look to figure 15.2, we can see how traders may use price action to predict a reversal in the direction of the market. The chart below is snapshot showing 5 days' worth of market movements (each bar represents a day). In the week leading up to this, the market had been in a downtrend (the price dropping). The 1st bar on the left was a big bearish bar showing the sellers dominating on that day, as they had been for the last week. The 2nd bar however has a small wick and a small body, meaning the sellers and the buyers were well matched on the next day and the price didn't fluctuate as much. This is referred to as an indecision bar. The market on the 3rd day opened at point A, the sellers brought it all the way down to point C, but the buyers pulled

178

the price back up to point B. This is a sign of a potential trend reversal. They did the same thing on the 4th day. These bars with long downward wicks are called low tests. In this case there was a double low test, on day three and four. On the 5th day we see the start of a trend reversal, with the market opening at point A, and the bulls dominating. Closing of the day at point B with a big increase in price. This is an example of how traders use price action to make buy/sell decisions.

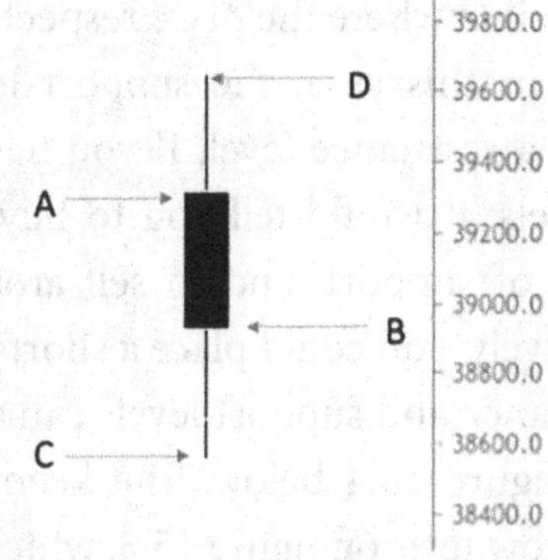

Figure 15:1: A candlestick bar.

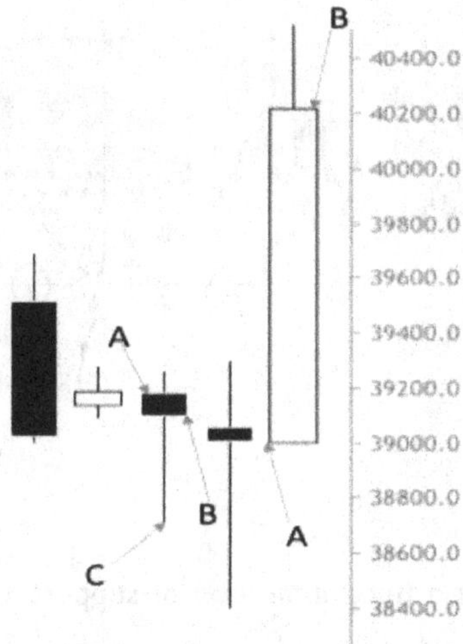

Figure 15:2: 5-day Candlestick chart.

Levels of Support and Resistance

Levels of support and resistance are horizontal or diagonal lines that the stock price doesn't seem to cross, changing direction once it reaches them. These levels act as a floor or a ceiling for the share price to follow. The example you see in figure 15.3 shows a horizontal level, where the price appears to respect. You can see two instances where the price respected the support level (the floor), and two of points where the price respected the resistance level (the ceiling). In this case, the support level was broken and is now used as a resistance level. If you have confidence in your horizontal levels, it would tell you to buy when the price is around the level of support, and to sell around the level of resistance. Alternatively, you could place a short trade at the level of resistance. Resistance and support levels can also be diagonal, as is visible from figure 15.4 below. The keen eyed may have noticed the double low tests on figure 15.3, which coincided with the level of support and a reversal in price action.

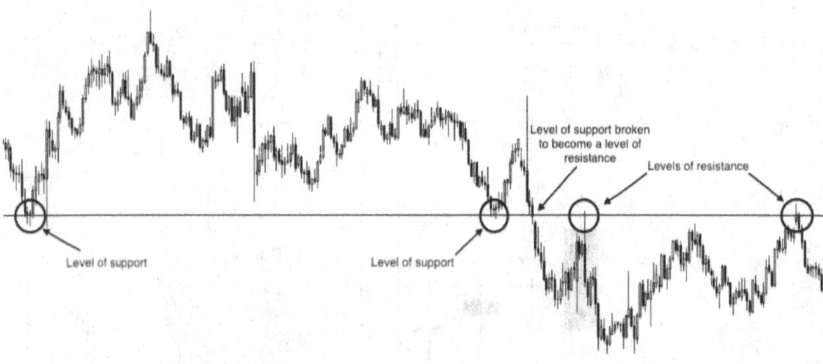

Figure 15:3: The use of a horizontal level of support and resistance with a candlestick chart.

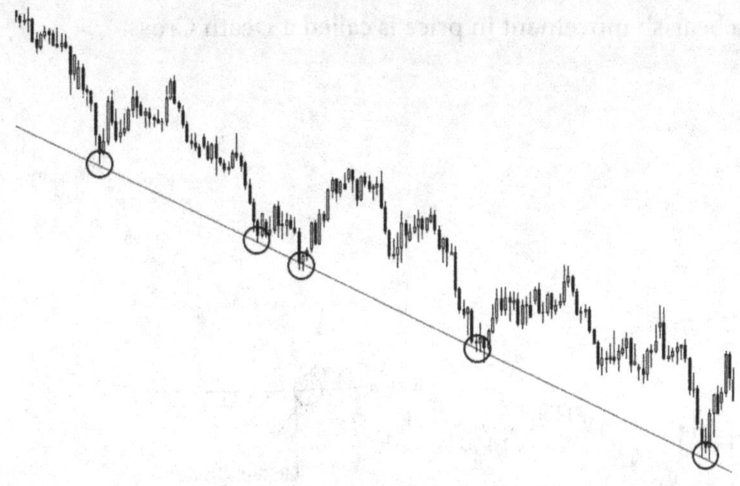

Figure 15:4: The use of a diagonal level of support in a downtrend.

Moving Averages

A moving average uses the mean of the price of a stock over a specified time period. The common time periods used are 20-day, 50-day and 200-day moving averages. Moving averages can be plotted on a graph, and can be used as levels of support and resistance as discussed above. They can also be compared to one another, as we will discuss below.

Below in figure 15.5, is a chart containing a 20-day and 200-day moving average. The price respects the 200 moving average as a level of support. This changes when the price breaks through the 200-day moving average. At this point you then see a crossover, which is knows as a Golden Cross. This is when the shorter time frame (20-day) moving average crosses and rises above the longer time frame (200-day) moving average. The Golden Cross is a bullish signal (if it wasn't obvious in the name). In figure 15.5, we can see the market starting an uptrend after this bullish signal. If you think the Golden

Cross is a lame term, the term for the opposite crossover that leads to a bearish movement in price is called a Death Cross.

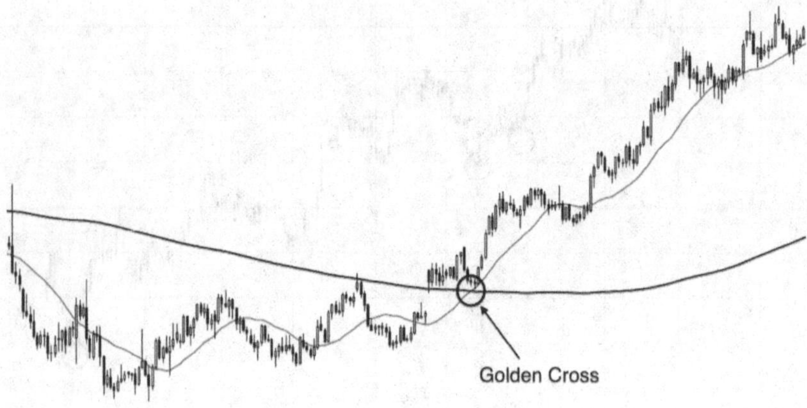

Figure 15:5: A candlestick chart showing the 20-day moving average (thinner line) crossing over the 200-day moving average (thicker line) forming a Golden Cross.

This is but a few of the indicators that constitute technical analysis. There are many more, including one that uses the Fibonacci sequence, believe it or not. If any of you looking at this think it is complete nonsense, then know that you are not alone. There are people who make a lot of money doing this, but you have to be very disciplined and have excellent risk tolerance. With technical trading you are relying on volume, in particular having the number of winning trades exceed that of the losing ones. Be assured, you will definitely have a lot of losing trades. A trader must ensure that the losses from these losing trades are minimised. This is where good risk management and the use of stop losses become crucial. If you want to read about investors that use technical analysis successfully, I recommend a book by Jack Schwager called *Market Wizards*.

Chapter 16
Savings, Compounding and Fiscal Prudence

Most finance books will talk about saving a portion of your earnings and investing to generate a return. If you want to read about this, then I recommend the *The Richest Man in Babylon* by George Samuel Clason. To summarise, one should put aside a percentage of what they earn every month. The trick is to take the money BEFORE all other expenses are taken out. The cut should be taken directly from the pay cheque. A lot of people do it the wrong way round, spending first and saving what they have left. Often, they find that after their 'necessary' expenses, there is no money left over for savings. If you save first, then you will control your spending, as that money will not physically exist in the account. Doing it this way round will make you realise that the £5 Starbucks coffee on the way to work will no longer be the necessity you thought it was.

The second things finance books all talk about is compounding. Compounding refers to taking the money you earn from investing, and reinvesting this to accumulate more over time. To explain with an example, your end-of-month pay cheque comes to £2,500. You have decided to save 20% of your pay cheque. You take the £500 (20% x £2,500), and invest it in Vodafone. They pay a 10% dividend annually, so after one year you make £50 (10% x £500). Instead of spending this, you sign up to a dividend reinvestment scheme, which invests this £50 back into Vodafone stock. The next year you make 10% again, not on the original £500, but on the increased £550. The next year, you make £55 (10% x £550). You reinvest this and next year make £66.55. If you compounded for ten years, your £500 would become £1,297. If you had chosen to not reinvest the dividend in a benefit from compounding, then after ten years you would have been left with £1,000. Now the extra £297 achievable via the compounding method may not seem like a lot, but it is 30% more than if you had not compounded. If you had invested £20,000 into Vodafone, then compounding would leave you with £11,874 more. Bear in mind, this doesn't take into account increases in share price over the ten years, which with compounding, would create an even bigger difference when compared to a non-compounded approach.[1]

Fiscal prudence is all about making sure the taxman takes as little of your gains as possible. In the US you have the 401k, and in the UK you have ISAs. Both these funds allow tax-free returns on investments. In the UK you can put up to £20k into an ISA every year. Any capital gains or dividend on this money is tax deductible. Otherwise, you are paying capital gains tax and dividend tax. With a LISA (lifetime ISA), every year you can put up to £4k and get 25% free from the government. So, if you put in the full £4k, you get £1k free! Note that if you do this, you can

---

1 Over ten years of compounding, a 20% annual return yields 2.38 times what a 10% annual return does (when one would expect it to return two times – as it would for the non-compounded model). In this way returns for compounding are non-linear. The bigger the compounded percentage yield, the bigger the discrepancy.

only put a maximum of £16k into your ISA to make the total £20k limit mentioned earlier (£4k LISA + £16k ISA = £20k). This is an amazing way to make tax-free returns. If you don't take your money out, then you can allow it to compound year on year.

Remember, things only get taxed when gains are realised. By this I mean when the share is sold and the money is in your account. By holding a share, you allow the money you have to grow without being taxed. Let me give you two examples to explain this. Let's say you buy company A, you invest £1,000 and make a 20% yield after one year. Then you sell it for a price of £1,200, incur capital gains tax of 20%, meaning your yield goes to 16% and your end sum is £1,160. You then invest that money into stock B which gives you a 10% yield after the second year. This 10% will act on the post-tax figure of £1,160, which takes your total to £1,276. You haven't sold this share yet, so you haven't incurred any capital gains, leaving you with a share worth £1,276.

Let's flip the scenario and say you invest in Company A and receive the same 20% return after the first year, leaving you with the share worth £1,200. Instead of selling it and incurring tax, you leave the money invested with Company A for the second year, which generates the same 10% return that Company B gave. This brings your end of second year share value to £1,320.

In the second scenario, you are not paying tax on your capital gains, utilising the whole £1,200 to generate more returns. For the first scenario, due to the penalty incurred through tax, Company B would have to yield 14% to get the same £1,320 figure as the second scenario. Whenever we decide to sell and buy another company, we have to factor this into the equation. We must consider not only whether better prospects lie in a different company, but whether those prospects are good enough to beat the capital gains tax dilemma discussed above.

The same goes with companies paying out dividends. They have to pay company tax on it themselves, then we as shareholders pay dividend tax. It's taxed twice! For this reason, if the company, instead of paying out money to shareholders, uses it themselves to cause company growth and hence share price increase, then I am more than happy for them not to pay out dividends. When a company uses the money irresponsibly, as mentioned in Chapter 5, then I would rather they pay a dividend, for me to invest as I chose.

Whatever country you are based in, I recommend you look into tax-free schemes like the ISAs and 401ks. They are a great way to avoid the issues with tax discussed above. It's really worthwhile finding a good accountant that is savvy with ways to reduce taxes incurred from investments. A practice I utilise with my accountant is tax loss harvesting. This gave me the ability to materialise losses in my stock portfolio, as I was able write this off against my other capital gains or taxable income. This means that my capital gains or income appears as 'lower' by the amount lost on the investment, so the tax bill was also lower. It was a good way to get rid of some losing investments I no longer wanted to own. These are the kind of things your accountant should be telling you, instead of just doing the bare minimum that most do.

Chapter 17
Case Studies

How to Find Investments

A common question my students ask is, now that I know how to analyse a stock, how do I find them? Finding the stock is the start of the investment process, so it is something that needs to be covered before we go through the case studies. Unfortunately, there is no straightforward answer to this question. My advice to all investors is to prime their environment for the generation of investment ideas. These ideas can come from multiple sources, ranging from your own shopping habits to the financial news. The former is not to be underestimated and is a part of Peter Lynch's philosophy.[1] Your own observations can be a potent source of ideas, so you now need to start keeping your eyes open for potential investment opportunities. I was climbing in Zhangjiajie, in the Avatar Mountains, and on top there was a queue for Starbucks! It made me think about how amazing a business it is. It sells a legal addictive substance, which people clearly can't get enough of. Not only is their coffee overpriced, but it also isn't even that good. That clearly doesn't stop people. What initiated my analysis into Starbucks was the huge queues I witnessed at their drive-through during COVID lockdowns. It was as big as the McDonald's drive-through queue, which is the business I ended up investing in instead. I should have bought both!

Another way to gain information is through social media. Following investing accounts on your Instagram or X accounts is a good way to keep in the loop and learn about potential new ideas. For those of you who like podcasts, there are plenty of investing podcasts that focus on current affairs that can provide ideas.

Subscriptions to investment research groups and newsletters can be another source of information. These are people who are experts and put out market research on a range of different asset classes. There are some that specialise in a particular asset class, or ones that cover lots of different areas of the market. The downside to all of these is that they are normally paid subscriptions. For paid subscription newsletters that will give you a good general overview, I recommend Wall Street Journal and Bloomberg. For a free resource, Yahoo Finance is an excellent place to start.

Lastly, I would recommend forming a group of like-minded individuals. In self-help books it is often referred to as a 'mastermind group.' These are people with whom you can share your ideas, discuss potential investments and come up with new strategies. It's a: 'sum of the whole is greater than that of its parts.'[1]

Once we have the idea, we need to do an analysis of the share. The analysis we carry out will depend on why we are buying the share. If we are buying a company for its bonds, the analysis will be different than if we were to buy it for growth. The stock we are going to analyse together is a stock I bought as a value buy. The company is American Express, known as AMEX. I will go through the qualitative and quantitative analysis that drove me to purchase the stock.

---

1 You can read about this in One Up on Wall Street.

Case Study 1 – American Express

QUALITATIVE ASSESSMENT

In 2020 it was prime COVID lockdown. The country had effectively shut down, and the stock market had taken a hit. This proved to be prime time for a contrarian investor such as myself, as most stocks were trading at a discount to their pre-COVID prices. Utilising this rare opportunity, I wanted to pick up blue-chip stocks at a discount.

American Express is a good company for a few reasons. Firstly, they have a higher credit quality than other banks. In uncertain times such as COVID, the risk of a recession was a concern with lockdowns. As AMEX serve a more affluent client base, their loans are at a lower risk of default. Also, in a recession, the middle class is affected less than the working class, so their spending habits wouldn't be as affected.

Secondly, they have a very strong brand identity. It's a brand that people aspire to obtain. Brand power is a very powerful quality, and is the reason its users pay $550 annually for an AMEX Platinum card.

Finally, its earnings don't just come from loans, but its payment transaction service. Like Visa and Mastercard, it takes a percentage transaction fee every time we use AMEX cards. AMEX actually charges a higher transaction fee to vendors than the latter two companies.

These reasons were enough for me to justify delving into the financials of the company.

QUANTITATIVE ASSESSMENT (2019 ANNUAL REPORT)

1. Balance Sheet

AMEX have:

Cash and cash equivalents = $23,932 million

These easily cover their short-term obligations:

Short-term borrowings = $6,442 million
Accounts payable = $12,738 million

In their liability section you will see:

Customer deposits = $73,287 million

These are liabilities because they are owed to people who have money in AMEX bank accounts. Theoretically if everyone at AMEX decided they want to take their money out of AMEX, they would have a slight issue, in that they don't have enough in liquid assets to pay everyone back. This is what happens when you get a 'bank run.' If everyone wants to take their money out, the banks don't have the cash on hand. In this case the banks may go bankrupt. Bank runs were common in the 2008 financial crash, where too many people lost faith in the banking system and wanted to take their money out.[1]

On review of AMEX's balance sheet, they have good amounts in cash and cash equivalents, which easily cover their short-term

---

[1] This happened again in 2023. A run on bank caused Silicon Valley Bank, Signature Bank and First Republic Bank to go bankrupt.

liabilities. Their total assets – customer loans and other receivables – exceed their long-term debt. They are a well-established bank, and will be far down the list of banks to suffer from a 'bank run.'

2. Income Statement

The company earned:
Total revenue = $43,556 million

The company makes provisions for losses, which is a non-cash charge (will not affect cash flows) but is deducted from the income statement:

Provision for losses = $3,573 million
Total revenue = $39,983 million

It is always worth calculating a company's operating profit margin (OPM), to see how efficiently the company is run:

Net income = $6,759 million
Net OPM = 16.9%
Average Net OPM banks – 10-15%

Another way to calculate a bank's efficiency is their Return on Assets, or their ROA:

Return on assets = 3.4%
Average ROA for banks = 1.33%

For both markers of an efficient company, AMEX is above average.

To assess the growth of a company, calculate the CAGR, or

compounded annual growth rate (see Chapter 11):

CAGR for the past ten years = 12% per annum

This is an excellent growth rate which should be factored into the company's intrinsic value calculation, which at the time I didn't bother carrying out as I knew it was a great price. However, as I didn't have a set target, I ended up selling the company too early. By capturing early gains, I missed out on a big move in the share price.

3. Cash Flows

Net cash flow from operating activity = $13,632 million

This is double the company's net income. This higher figure is due to a number of non-cash charges that are subtracted in the calculation of income. An example of this is:

Provision for losses = $(3,573 million)
This is not a cash charge as no money has been 'lost' yet.

The company makes quite some outlays in the form of investments and new loans:

Purchase of investments = $(11,166 million)
Net increase in Card Member loans = $(11,047 million)

They also make some large payments to benefit shareholders:
Repurchase of American Express common shares = $(4,685 million)
Dividends paid = $(1,422 million)

In the end the net change in cash holdings:

Net (decrease) increase in cash and cash equivalents = $(3,362 million)

Their cash holdings are still plentiful:

Cash and cash equivalent (including restricted cash) = $24,446 million

4. Share Price

Share price = $93

Earning per share = $7.99

Price to Earnings Ratio = 8.6

Average P/E banks = 8.5

Average P/E of AMEX = 18.8

CONCLUSION

Based on the above calculations I decided that AMEX was an excellent business. I found both good qualitative and quantitative reasons to invest in the company. The drop in the share price gave me as a contrarian investor a good opportunity to pick a high-quality company at a reduced price. On reflection, my mistake in this investment, as mentioned above, was not having a set intrinsic value calculation. This led to me to selling the stock early to capture the 43.8% gains made that year. However, I missed out on the near 100% return I could have achieved had I calculated intrinsic value and had a more strategical end point for my investment.

TASK – Calculate an estimated intrinsic value for AMEX at the end of 2019. If you want to use the financial metric method, then you can use the data above.

Case Study 2 - Disney

Another stock I bought at the same time as AMEX was Disney. Let's do the same qualitative and quantitative assessment as above.

QUALITATIVE ASSESSMENT

I first found out about the drop in Disney stock from the news reporting a negative outlook for the company due to its nationwide theme park closure. As a contrarian this presented an opportunity to invest in what I knew to be an excellent company.

Disney have incredible branding power. The Disney brand is iconic, which extends to hundreds of different characters, appealing to all age groups, each of which can be monetised in a whole host of different ways, from T-shirts and figurines to theme parks and cruises. They also have a plethora of content, and are constantly bringing out spin-offs and sequels to further the brand's reach. I see more and more adults getting into Disney shows than I remember being the case as a child.

Indeed, the theme parks were closed, but lockdown wouldn't go on forever and Disney theme parks are heaven on earth for children. Every child dreams of going to Disneyland, to see their favourite characters in the flesh.

Investors were also concerned about the closure of cinemas. However, the company just released a new streaming platform, Disney+. In lockdown, streaming content was the hot business to get into, with everyone staying indoors with not much to do. What impressed me was the initiative from the management team to diversify into streaming, a sector in which Disney, with all film content already made, was well positioned to succeed.

TASK – I had actually written out the quantitative analysis of Disney, then I decided to remove it, sorry … The reason I did this is that you have all the tools to do it yourself! The last task of the book is to do the same quantitative analysis for Disney that we did for AMEX above. For those of you that skipped all the other tasks, this is the one you don't want to miss. You may use any financial year you want. The pointers below are for the 2019 annual report. You may want to use the most recent year, however, as you can use the analysis and assess whether it is a good time to invest in the company. For help with the calculations, you might need to flick back to Chapters 6 and 11. Here are the pointers for the 2019 annual report:

1. **Balance sheet**
    You will find that the company has a negative working capital (see Chapter 6). As the company has a very dependable income, it can maintain higher levels of short-term debt than its current assets can cover.

2. **Cash Flows**
    You will see a discrepancy in net income and cash flow. If you look at the *Provision for income tax*, the company pays a huge tax bill that year (eleven times more than the previous year).

3. **Cash Flows**
    The company refinances its debt, see the *Borrowings* and *Reduction of borrowings* row. They show $38 billion of cash influx from borrowing, and $38 billion cash outlay from reduction of borrowing.

4. **Cash Flows**
    They spend $9.9 billion on *Acquisitions*, but do no *Repurchases of common stock* and pay *Dividends* of $2.9 billion, which is a low yield.

Chapter 18
Finding Your Own Style

I wanted to put this chapter at the end, as although it doesn't have as much information and facts as the other chapters, it contains a crucial take-home message: that you can learn from the greats of investing, but you have to find your own style. If you mindlessly copied a famous investor's buys, then you have to know why they are buying that stock. If you don't know why the stock was bought, you will never know when to sell. You will not know when to cut your losses, or when to capture your gains.

The second point is that no one can predict the future with certainty. Even the best investors in the world regularly get it wrong. Their trick is maximising the upside on the winners and minimising the downside on the losers. This is all part of good risk management, which we mentioned in Chapter 9.

The third reason is that everyone's investing horizon is different, so they make different decisions with their own wealth. If you have a family and want to leave your children something, then you would have a very different portfolio from a younger investor wanting to chase higher and riskier returns. Your financial position also has an impact on investing style. If you have a large cash flow after expenses, then you may want to invest with more risk. Finally, your mental make-up also plays a part. Some people are risk-averse. It increases stress, causes sleepless nights and effects mental well-being. This is one of the reasons I don't technical trade, as it causes me too much stress.

I have gone over lots of different investment styles, and it's a lot to digest, but becoming an investor is a process which will take time and unfortunately mistakes will be made. Hopefully, you have learnt from some of my errors shared in this book, so you don't make the same ones. I have also shared some of the investments I have made, and by the time you are reading this, you will know if they were good decisions. The reason I shared recent decisions I made is because the decision-making process is extremely important. Of course, the result is also important, but bear in mind that a poor result doesn't necessarily mean poor decision making. There is always the presence of the unknown, which can hinder or help your investment. The important thing is factoring in the risk of the unknown, and having a contingency plan if things don't go your way.

I'll now share my portfolio make-up and what I invest in. Currently, we are at risk of a recession due to rising interest rates and high inflation. For this reason, I have 20% of my portfolio in cash. I keep this so I have funds ready to deploy when conditions ripen. 31% is in my fixed income portfolio, which is focused on stocks to hold for the long run. These stocks belong to excellent businesses, with good free cash flow and generous but sustainable dividends. 19% of my portfolio is held in riskier investments. A portion is in gold and silver mines, which alongside bitcoin, serve as my risk-on inflation hedges.[1] Last but not least, I have investments in real estate, which encompasses the remaining 30% of my portfolio.

I roughly follow the rule of thirds. One third in marketable

---

1 A 'risk-on' asset is one which carries a higher risk, with the aim of achieving a higher return. Typically these are investments with a greater amount of price volatility.

securities, one third in real estate and one third in liquid assets. I'm not telling you about my portfolio because I think it is something you should follow. I included it for those of you who are curious about my own investment decisions. I think it is important to know the author's decisions, as they also give an idea of the author's investment philosophy. Although I've tried to be as objective as possible in this book, my bias has inevitably creeped in. I'll end with a quote from Gustave Flaubert: "There is no truth. There is only perception."

Good luck investing!

Glossary

Acquisition – The process when one company buys all or parts of another company.

Active Investing – Investing in a selection of securities from the market with the hope of 'beating the market' and generating alpha (see above).

Alpha – The return a portfolio has delivered in excess of the general market's rate of return over the same time period. It's a measure of how well an investor has performed relative to a benchmark (usually the S&P).

Amortisation – Process of gradually writing off the cost of an asset during its 'shelf life'.

Appreciation – The increase in the value of an asset.

Ask Price – The minimum price a seller is willing to accept for a security.

Asset – An item which has economic value. This can be a stock, real estate or any item that has monetary value.

Base Interest Rate – The interest rate that the central bank will charge other banks and building societies for loans.

Through this, central banks can increase or decrease the money supply flowing into the economy.

Bearish – A term pertaining to a downward movement in price. A 'bearish' signal is a signal suggesting the asset with a decrease in price.

Bears – Refer to group of individuals selling a security.

Beta – The measure of volatility of an asset or portfolio. Can be used to quantify the level of risk of a portfolio.

Bid Price – The highest price a buyer will pay for a security

Blue-Chip – Relating to a stock of a high-quality company. One that is considered very financially stable and is highly reputable. Examples include Amazon, Apple, Microsoft, Walmart etc.

Bond – A debt instrument which represents a loan from the investor to the company, on which interest is paid to the investor.

Bottom-up Approach – Investing based on analysis of an individual stock as opposed to macroeconomic factors.

Bubble – An escalation in the price of a group of assets, usually priced at a figure well above their intrinsic worth.

Bullish – The opposite of bearish, indicating upward movement in price.

Bulls – refer to a group of individuals buying a security.

Call Option – A leveraged financial instrument, used to multiply gains when the price of the share increases.

Capital Gains – Profit acquired from the sale of an investment or property.

Commodities – Raw materials or agricultural products.

Examples include corn, coffee, copper .

Convertible – The ability to convert an asset, for example a bond or preferred share, into common shares.

Coupon – The interest rate that is promised to the bondholders (see Bond).

Cryptocurrency – A digital currency where transactions are verified by a decentralised system.

DCF (Discounted Cash Flow) – A methodology used to calculate a company's intrinsic value.

Depreciation – the opposite of appreciation, the decrease in value of an asset.

Dividend – A payment of a portion of the company's profits to its shareholders.

Downtrend – A reduction in the price of a security over time, characterised by lower highs and lower lows.

Equities – Entities that represent a stake/share in a company. Stocks for example are equities that are tradable on a public stock exchange.

ETFs (Exchange-Traded Funds) – A bundle of assets and securities (see Securities) that can be bought to aid diversification.

Fiat Money – Government issued currency that is not backed by a physical asset such as gold.

Fiscal – Relating to government revenue, including taxes.

Futures – Leveraged financial instruments that allow an investor to multiply gains from increases or decreases in the price of a commodity (see Commodities).

Headwind – Used to describe conditions that inhibit progress and can lead to a decrease in value or growth of a company or economy.

Hedging – A risk management strategy employed to reduce losses in investments by making investments in an opposing position to the main investment.

Index – A way to measure the performance of a broad group of assets of a certain sector. One cannot invest directly into an index, they may do so indirectly using an index fund (see below).

Index Fund – An ETF (see above) which contains all the assets contained within the particular index. Allows an investor to indirectly invest into an index.

Indexing – A passive form of investing which aims to replicate the performance of an index (see above).

Inflation – The increase in prices as a result of the decrease in purchasing power of money

Interest Rates – The interest payable on borrowings and loans.

Large-cap – Large-caps refer to companies with 'large capitalisation'. These are companies with market capitalisations of $10 billion or above (see Mid-caps and Small-caps below). Often institutional investors have limits on what they can purchase. A pension fund manager for example, may only be able to purchase Large-caps, as they are on the whole, a safer asset class then Small-caps.

Leveraging – The use of borrowed capital to maximise one's profits.

Liabilities – The financial obligations of a company.

Liquidation – In the process of bankruptcy, the company sells off (liquidates) its assets and pays off its liabilities.

Liquidity – How easily an asset can be converted into cash.

Macroeconomics – The study of the economy as a whole, studying phenomena which have a widespread effect such as inflation, interest rates, unemployment etc.

Market Capitalisation – The total value of a company traded on the stock market (share price x number of shares).

Market Liquidity – The ability of an individual to sell or buy shares without causing large changes in the price of the share.

Marketable Security – Financial assets that can be bought on the public market.

Mergers – When two or more companies combine to form a new company.

Mid-cap – A company with a market capitalisation between $2 and $10 billion.

Options – Leveraged financial instruments used to multiply any gains made either from bullish (call options) or bearish (puts) price action.

Passive Investing – Maximising return by minimising the amount of buying/selling and holding for a longer time frame. The most common form of passive investing is indexing (see above).

Precious Metals – The four main precious metals are gold, silver, platinum and palladium.

Preferred Shares – These shares have a fixed dividend and have priority over common shares.

Price Action – The movement of a security's price over time

Puts – The opposite of call options. A leveraged instrument used to multiply returns when the asset decreases in price.

Repurchases (Shares) – The company buying back its own outstanding shares, the increase shareholder equity for the remaining shareholders.

Risk-off Asset – Investments that are of a lower risk, prioritising capital preservation. Typically an investor would be more risk-off in unfavourable market conditions.

Risk-on Asset – Investments that carry a higher risk with the aim of achieving a higher return. Typically an investor would be more risk-on in favourable market conditions.

ROA – Return on assets. A measure of efficiency, analysing how much a company can generate on the assets it owns.

Security – A valuable asset with monetary value which is able to be traded.

Shareholder Equity – The assets attributable to the shareholders. It is calculated by subtracting the total assets from the total liabilities.

Short Selling – Selling a stock which is not owned at the time, with the hope of purchasing it at a lower price later on. It is a way to profit from a decrease in asset price.

Small-cap – A company with a market capitalisation between $250 million and $2 billion.

SPAC – Special purpose acquisition company. A public company which raises capital with the intention of acquiring or merging (see above) with an existing company.

GLOSSARY

Speculation – Investing in an asset with the hope it will go up, using no strategy or risk management.

Spread – The difference between the Ask and the Bid price

Stock Exchange – A market where financial securities are bought and sold.

Stop Loss – An order to sell a security at a specific price to limit the loss suffered.

Tailwind – Used to describe conditions that may help stimulate and increase growth of a company or economy.

Technical Trading – The use of signals and historical patterns to predict future market movements.

Top-down Approach – Looking at the macroeconomic factors to make investment decisions before delving into company-specific factors.

Uptrend – An increase in the price of a security over time, characterised by higher highs and higher lows.

Volatility – The amount of upward or downward movement of a security (see Beta).

Warrants – An instrument that gives the holder the right to buy or sell a security.

Yield – The return on an investment, normally expressed as a percentage.

Author Bio

Qasim is a real estate investment trust manager and dentist, whose passion in life is finance and economics. He got into the market at a young age, starting his trading journey on the foreign exchange market. After falling in love with investing, he went on to attend courses and obsessively read books, articles and shareholder letters. His investing style is influenced by the works of some of the great value investors to which he has referred throughout the book. He has loved teaching since his first ever job as a chemistry tutor, and after witnessing the impact that investing made on his life, he wanted to help others take control of their financial future. When teaching investing, he found that the books he would recommend were either too complex or too simple. *From Speculator to Investor* is an effort to bridge that gap.